HOW TO MARKET A CHILDREN'S BOOK

CHILDREN'S PRINT BOOK, EBOOK AND AUDIOBOOK MARKETING, TRANSLATIONS AND SELLING FOREIGN RIGHTS

KAREN P INGLIS

Published by Well Said Press 2021

83 Castelnau . London . SW13 9RT

Paperback ISBN: 978-1-913846-03-9

ePub ISBN: 978-1-913846-04-6

CONTENTS

INTRODUCTION

Welcome to *How to Market a Children's Book*

Thank you for buying this book, and congratulations if you have a children's story out in the world — or if you have just self-published (or had published) your first story. *How to Market a Children's Book* is dedicated to helping you make the most of every opportunity out there to promote your story and get it into young readers' hands.

If you've been self-publishing for a while, you will be all too aware of the marketing challenges we children's authors face. The opportunities we have — and the pathways to our readers — differ from what's available to authors who write for adult or even young adult (YA) audiences, because our readers are not online in the places where we carry out most of our marketing. And even where they are, there are strict data protection rules that prevent us from promoting to them directly.

That means we need to do some things differently and put in more time and more thought. It is hard work — but there are strategies you can implement, both offline and online, that will serve you well. Some are 'old school' approaches — and the power of these is not to be underestimated for establishing your brand. Others are more advanced — based around social media, email marketing and advertising platforms. For each of these approaches, there is a growing number of fantastic tools out there that will help you spread your message.

This book aims to round up what you need to know in one place — starting from the beginning, if that's where you are, while allowing those further into their marketing journey to jump to more advanced marketing tasks.

If you have a great children's story (appropriate in terms of theme, length and use of language for its target audience, and that has been professionally edited and illustrated), there is no reason why you shouldn't be able to get it into the hands of hundreds or even thousands of children at home and abroad. I hope to help you achieve that.

Note: For those of you who have the **first edition** of *'How to Self-publish and Market a Children's Book'*, you will find that what follows is a greatly expanded version of the content of the second part of that book. Clearly, much of the marketing information from that first publication was evergreen — and, to that extent, some of the content you will find here is the same. However, there are many new sections and more in-depth information in previous existing chapters, not least when it comes to social media marketing, advertising, and school visits. I hope you find this additional information useful.

As you are probably aware, this is a 'sibling' publication of the much larger *'How to Self-publish and Market a Children's Book (Second Edition)'*. I intend to split the larger book into two when significant updates on the self-publishing side are next needed. In the meantime, this marketing edition now and in the future aims to meet the needs of self-publishers who are up to speed with the self-publishing process itself.

1

MY MARKETING JOURNEY

The figures and anecdotes I share below demonstrate what is possible if you are prepared to put in the hard work after your story goes to print. All figures are as at the end of March 2021. (I should add that I know of plenty of self-published children's authors who have outsold me.)

Note that I am deliberately including the smaller wins with the obvious big one with *The Secret Lake,* because I recognise it to be an outlier. Hopefully, the anecdotes below will show how little things can often lead to bigger things for each book. It's also worth noting that the 'smaller win' figures are still very respectable when compared with sales for many traditionally published 'midlist' (not bestseller) children's books.

As I said in the introduction, if you have a great story that was rigorously planned and published following editorial best practice for children's titles, whilst you may not necessarily replicate some of these numbers, you still have a good chance of selling hundreds if not thousands of books.

The Secret Lake

- Over 250,000 sales in print (English language)
- Almost 20,000 Kindle / eBook sales
- Over 8,000 audiobook sales
- Praised by librarians, teachers, reading charities and parents for its manageable length and being used as class readers in UK and US schools
- Considered for adaptation by Children's BBC TV after being read by CBBC Head of Independent Commissioning
- Foreign rights sold in seven countries
- Over 9,000 Amazon global ratings/ reviews
- Managed translation into German in 2020; as I write 5,000 print sales since publication (Sept 2020) and *Amazon.de* bestseller badges in key categories

Eeek! The Runaway Alien

- Over 3,000 print sales
- Selected as *LoveReading4Kids* Book of the Month at publication (a highly regarded UK children's book recommendation site)
- Used for Years 2 and 3 literacy projects (2012, 2013, 2016)
- Unsolicited requests for school visits
- Received over £450 in royalties from schools' copying

- Requests for reading copies from mainstream publishers in Turkey and Germany
- Used in the *Get London Reading* campaign in 2014

Ferdinand Fox's Big Sleep

- Over 900 print sales
- Shipped 17 copies to Cyprus in 2018 following a Skype school visit request — this led to later virtual visits with subsequent picture books

Ferdinand Fox and the Hedgehog

- Over 3,000 print sales
- One online purchase led to two whole-school visits

Henry Haynes and the Great Escape

- Over 3,000 print sales
- Extremely popular with early readers!

Walter Brown and the Magician's Hat

- Over 2,000 print sales
- Red Ribbon Winner, Wishing Shelf Book Awards 2016 (judged by children and teachers in six UK primary schools)

The Christmas Tree Wish (Oct 2019)

- Over 2,000 print sales — seasonal marketing only
- Shortlisted for the 2020 UK 'Selfies Award' for best self-published children's book
- Over 1,000 sales of the French edition (*Martin le Sapin de Nöel)*
- Over 70 sales of the German edition (*Chris Christbaums Weihnachtstraum)*

The Tell-Me Tree (July 2020)

- Over 2,500 print sales
- Praise from both parents and schools who are using it to help children share feelings
- As I write, over 300 likes, 170 shares and 130 comments on a UK Facebook Ad I created to promote it — my first ever successful Facebook ad!

Making a living from my books

In the last couple of years I can finally say that I've been making a *good* living from my books, running into six figures. Until then — and after a lot of hard work and learning — I was earning a *reasonable* income. This had gradually risen to around £1,000 a month by late 2017.

If you're prepared to work hard, you could achieve results on this spectrum — just don't give up the day job unless you can afford to! According to a 2018 survey[1] commissioned by the Authors Licensing and Collecting Society (ALCS), the median annual income of UK 'primary occupation' professional writers (including authors) was below £10,500 in 2018 — a drop of 42% in real terms since 2006 and around 15% since 2013. There is no further breakdown, but I wouldn't be surprised if that income figure was quite a bit lower for the average midlist traditionally published children's author. As at April 2021 there are no more recent figures — and, while I know good numbers of self-published authors who are now bucking the trend, it took them a lot of time and effort to get there.

Finding success, particularly as a children's author, is hard work and a steady, slow-burn process. The fact you are reading this book tells me you are in for the long haul, which means you are one step ahead already.

---

1. 'UK Authors' Earnings and Contracts 2018' : UK Copyright and Creative Economy Centre, Glasgow University (commissioned by ALCS)

2

MARKETING PLANNING

Children's book buying facts and figures

Before diving into marketing practicalities, I thought it would be useful to start with an overview of children's book buying in the UK. Knowledge is power after all! These statistics will be useful to refer back to later as you develop your marketing plan.

Note: the figures that follow are from Nielsen UK's Monthly Books & Consumers Survey of Buying Habits in 2019. Clearly, book buying habits changed during 2020 as a result of the Covid-19 pandemic, with many more purchases happening online. UK statistics for 2020 are not available at the time of writing, and it is unclear to what degree habits will change back once lockdown is lifted permanently.

If new figures become available I will include them in an online resources folder associated with this book. (See Chapter 21 for how to access this.)

UK children's print book purchases 2019

Source: Nielsen UK's Monthly Books & Consumers Survey of Buying Habits in 2019

Children's UK book buying by format in 2019

- Print – 94%
- eBook – 3%
- Audiobook – 3%

Place of print children's book purchase

- Online – 39% (cf 72% for adult fiction / 59% adult non-fiction)
- Offline – 61% (cf 28% for adult fiction / 41% adult non-fiction)

Volume sales children's books by gender split

- Females accounted for 65% of children's books volume sales (cf 59% for all books)
- Males accounted for 35%. (cf 41% for all books)

Children's Book Discovery

- Word of mouth – 8%
- Browsing online – 10%
- Recipient asked for it – 14%
- Browsing offline (bookshops /elsewhere) – 15%
- Had read others by author/ in the series – 19%

I don't have a breakdown of 'Shops/elsewhere' from the above figures, but Nielsen's 2015 consumer survey figures may give some indication. At that time, they showed offline purchases as coming from the sources below, with the balance coming from online:

- 23.5% Chain bookshops
- 5.4% Other bookshops
- 13.6% Supermarkets
- 5% Bargain bookshops
- 16.9% A mix of non-specialist shops/venues/gift shops/department stores and mail order

Note that school event sales are not tracked by Nielsen.

Reasons for buying children's books

When asked why they bought children's books the reasons given in 2019 were:

- 'liked the series' – 21.1%.
- 'recipient asked' 'likes this author' /'likes this kind of book' – each round 18%
- 'interested in the subject' – 17.4%
- 'cover' and 'character(s') - each around 14%
- 'description' – around 12%
- 'Recommendation/review' –8.3%
- 'Look inside/extract' – around 7%

Note how important it is to establish your brand as a children's author, as buying relies heavily on children and their parents knowing who you are and on children's word of mouth (correlating to 'recipient asked') rather than on customer reviews.

CHILDREN'S BOOKS VOLUME SALES BY AGE RANGE OF BUYER

- 24% - buyer aged 13-24
- 25% - buyer aged 25-34
- 24% - buyer aged 35-44
- 15% - buyer ages 45-49
- 11% - buyer aged 60-84

What does children's book buying behaviour mean for indie authors?

You will see that while most children's books are bought 'offline' a large percentage are bought online in the UK. This is good news for indie authors and something you'll be able to tap into using online advertising platforms and social media. I'll be covering these topics later on.

To start with, however, most of your sales are likely to be offline and at face-to-face events, and this is what you need to prepare for at the start of your marketing. Don't see this as a chore, or be afraid — meeting your readers is one of the most rewarding things about being a children's author! And it's the start of the process that will gradually get you known through word of mouth — one of the key ways that children's books get discovered and recommended by parents, children, librarians and teachers. It's also extremely helpful for getting early reviews — and you will need these once you get to online marketing.

Your 10-Step Book Marketing Plan

In order to build your 'brand' and your confidence as an author, it's easiest and best to 'start local'. However, you need to have a couple of things in place beforehand that will support your marketing effort. Below I set out a 10-step plan to help you focus on your key tasks for marketing your books. These are roughly but not rigidly in order, as some activities you will set up in parallel.

Key elements of your marketing plan

1. Include marketing links and messages (including email sign-up incentives) in your book's back matter.
2. Make sure your Amazon Author bio page is filled out in key markets— take a look at competitor authors' pages for ideas.
3. Create an online presence with a website or blog and include a mailing list sign-up.
4. Add social media now or later (or not at all if it's really not for you).
5. Approach local libraries, bookshops, schools, playgroups and any relevant visitor centres.
6. Contact local press / magazines / local community websites.
7. Research local events / fairs.
8. Provide a free copy of your book to your beta readers and ask for an honest review.
9. Research and approach children's book review sites / bloggers / individual reviewers, and research children's book Giveaway programmes.

10. Experiment with Amazon Advertising and research other advertising options.

Steps 1 and 2 are crucial, and should be in place before you start marketing — so I'll cover them below. We will then look at the core marketing tasks in the following chapters.

Optimise your book's front and back matter

You should have dealt with this already at the production stage, as mentioned briefly at the end of Part One. What follows should be obvious but I'm including it for completeness.

Your book's back matter pages (and in some cases front matter) offer the perfect place to grow your sales and engage readers. You can use them to:

- ask for a review
- tell readers more about you
- encourage newsletter sign-up
- promote other titles

Asking for a review

'There's no harm in asking,' as they say. Be sure to ask your readers to leave a review with the help of a grown-up. I tend to reserve a whole page for this on the first page they see at the end of the book. However, if you're squeezed for page count it could simply be a stand-out paragraph on your 'About the author page'. Do what works best for the design/format of your book.

See below for a form of words I've used in my books to ask for reviews.

Please write a review
Authors love hearing from their readers!

Please let Karen Inglis know what you thought about *The Secret Lake* by leaving a short review on Amazon or your other preferred online store. It will help other parents and children find the story.

(If you're under age 13, ask a grown-up to help you.)
Thank you!

Top tip: be sure not to give away any of the story's secrets!

About the author page

This is a chance for your readers to get to know you.

A short paragraph with some fun facts is enough — look at author bios in children's books in your genre and see which strike a chord. Ideally include a headshot (which will be in black and white unless it's a picture book) — I strongly believe that putting a face to a name will increase the chances of parents or young readers becoming advocates if they enjoyed your story. I have nothing to back this up though!

This is also a good page to mention your newsletter or email sign-up incentive — on which more in a moment.

• • •

Promoting other titles

If you have more than one book, include an 'Also by YOUR NAME' page to promote your other titles. The format you use will depend on how much room you have and/or how many extra pages you are happy to add. Clearly, with a picture book there is less flexibility to add extra pages than with a middle grade novel or chapter book where you can even include sample material from another book.

Ways you can include cross-promotion

- A simple bullet list of each book with title, target age range* and an engaging short blurb of a line or two at most. See the example overleaf from *Ferdinand Fox and the Hedgehog*.
- Repeat as above but add in a greyscale thumbnail cover image of each title with each entry (or use colour for colour picture books).
- Use either of the above but also add a sample chapter or two from one of the books listed as a bonus.
- In all cases include a friendly (easy to remember) link that readers can use to locate your book(s) online — be that your author website, your Amazon page or other preferred online store author page.

*If, like me, you write across a range of age-groups, ideally include which age range your different titles are for. Every little helps in my view.

Who knows — perhaps your reader on seeing the age ranges may suddenly remember a niece or godchild's upcoming birthday for whom one of your titles looks suitable?

I have used all of the approaches above — see screenshot below for an example from *Ferdinand Fox and the Hedgehog.*

Also by Karen Inglis

Ferdinand Fox's Big Sleep (3-5 yrs)
"Ferdinand Fox curled up in the sun, as the church of St Mary struck quarter past one..."
Another gentle rhyming fox tale, based on a true story.

Henry Haynes and the Great Escape (6-8 yrs)
A boy, a bossy boa, a VERY smelly gorilla - and a zoo escape!

Eeek! The Runaway Alien (7-10 yrs) *Laugh-out-loud funny!*
A soccer-mad alien comes to Earth for the World Cup!

Walter Brown and the Magician's Hat (7-10 yrs) *Award winner!*
A magic hat, a talking cat and escaped video monsters...!

The Secret Lake (8-11 yrs) *Karen's best seller. Considered for CBBC TV.*
A lost dog, a hidden time tunnel and secret lake take Stella and Tom to their home and the children living there 100 years ago.

Ideally include age range for listed books if they vary.

Encouraging mailing list sign-ups

Use your 'About the author' page to encourage mailing list sign-up by offering something as a free bonus for the children to enjoy. Depending on the target age range for your book this might be free posters/colouring sheets/crossword puzzles based on the book — or a bonus short story or character diary. With *Ferdinand Fox and the Hedgehog* I include a link to free posters for download, and with *The Secret Lake* to a poster of the front cover and a crossword based on the story.

Tips to remain compliant

- Word your sign-up message so that children under age 13 must ask a grown-up to sign up for them, or must get a grown-up's permission to sign up.

- Also make it clear that they are signing up to receive your newsletter — not just the free download. The GDPR rules that came into force in the EU in May 2018 are strict about this. You don't want to be seen to be misleading your readers or tricking them into joining your list. (The UK has retained these rules post-Brexit.)

I talk about the practicalities of mailing list sign-ups in more detail, with examples, in Chapter 7.

Email sign-up at the start of your book

You could optionally repeat the free download offer at the start of your book — to be sure it doesn't get missed. I only do this with my eBooks at the moment, but as I write I wonder why I've not tried it in my print books!

The 'look inside' previews for print books on Amazon tend to by-pass the front matter so it wouldn't be seen here. However, it *could* help drive more purchases from children or parents browsing in your local bookshop — especially if the free offer is for something engaging that's connected to the book, such as a crossword puzzle.

At worst it won't make a difference — and if they take a photo of the download link to get the free offer without buying your book they will need to join your mailing list anyway. This gives you a further chance to try to turn them into paying customers.

EBook cross-marketing links

The beauty of cross promoting with eBooks is that you can link your reader directly to your chosen landing page — be this your Amazon author page, your Amazon book sales page, a landing page on your website, or the sales/author page for your book on any other online store if your eBooks are 'wide' (meaning not just on Amazon). Be sure to make the most of this opportunity.

If you're a Mac user and have Vellum, setting up cross marketing links is especially easy if your books are wide, as you can input links to your sales pages on the different eBook stores all in one place. Vellum then creates separate files for the different stores.

. . .

Links to Amazon 'write a review page'

Some authors provide a link on their review request page that goes directly to the (lower level) page on Amazon where the customer can compose their review. I've personally not done this as it's a rather stark and uninspiring page to land on and could be confusing. Instead I link to my book's main sales page, which shows the book's thumbnail and description and lists the customer reviews at the top — I then hope/trust anyone who's chosen to go this far will work it out from there. Put yourself in the customer's shoes and do what feels right for you.

Claim and set up your Amazon Author page

Once you've published your book to Amazon and see it listed, click on your author name link. You'll find a link in the left-hand navigation bar that says 'Are you the author?' and invites you to visit Author Central. Follow this link and the simple instructions to claim and add your book(s) then upload an author photo and add your bio. At the time of writing, you can post your bio to the following countries:

- UK
- US
- France
- Germany
- Italy
- Spain
- Portugal
- Japan

I've posted my bio in English for each territory, on the basis that buyers of most of my books will need to understand English in any event. As I have a German edition of *The Secret Lake* that's doing well, I may have that bio translated into German but I've not had time to do this yet.

Aside from providing a priceless brand marketing space, another benefit of setting up this page is that it shows your sales rankings for each book over given time periods. You can also see reviews for each book/territory in one place via a dropdown, upload videos and (coming soon unless you have it already) link a blog to your US page. It looks as if more features will be added in the future. Visit my UK/US author pages to get a feel for how this all looks.

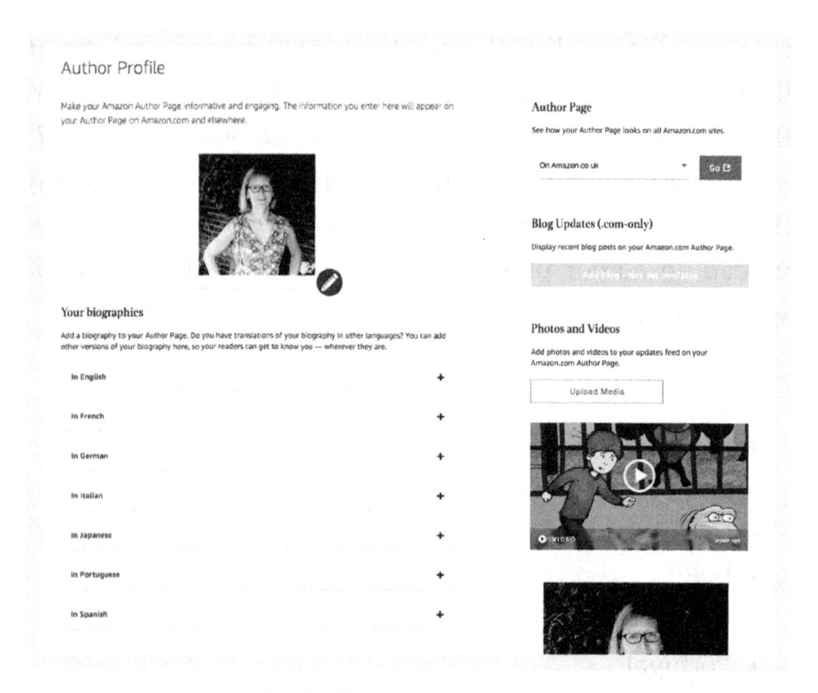

Your Amazon Author Profile page is quick and easy to set up and edit

3

AUTHOR WEBSITE: YOUR CALLING CARD

It goes without saying (I hope) that you need an online presence as an author. This doesn't mean you need to set up multiple social media accounts if that's not for you — or that you need to blog regularly. What it does mean is that, as a very minimum, you need an online 'calling card' to which you can refer bookshops, schools and other organisations you contact as part of your marketing plan.

I still have a clear memory of how useful it was for me when I contacted the Notting Hill branch of Waterstones (the UK's main high street book chain) back in 2011 just after *The Secret Lake* came out. Being able to refer the children's book buyer to my website in my initial email was crucial as it gave her additional context for the story, and a sense of my author 'brand'.

Because I self-publish with Ingram Spark as well as KDP, she could, of course, look the book up on her ordering system via its ISBN. However, she wouldn't have seen any further detail about my story beyond the title and cover. This is because, for UK-published titles, although Nielsen accepts and passes on the Ingram feed to most booksellers in the UK and worldwide, it blocks the book description unless you have paid for its Enhanced Service. The cost of this isn't a sensible use of a limited budget when starting out but becomes more feasible once you have several books out. (Google 'Nielsen's Enhanced Service' for more information.)

As well as being able to read *The Secret Lake's* plot summary on my website, the Waterstones book buyer could also read about the inspiration for the story (including its local connection) and learn more about me. I'd also been able to post some early reviews there. She was already suitably impressed by the time we spoke on the phone, and suggested I drop in to see her and bring a few copies. Waterstones in Notting Hill subsequently went on to stock and promote *The Secret Lake*. This, in turn, led to six more branches of Waterstones doing the same after I made contact — and led to many signing sessions over a three-year period, and over 200 books sold.

I hope this has convinced you that you need a website to refer book buyers and others to when you first get in touch.

Do you need a website for each book?

No. I don't recommend this even, though it's what I did when starting out. Create a single author site with your books clearly delineated. My separate sites for *The Secret Lake, Eeek! The Runaway Alien* and *The Adventures of Ferdinand Fox* quickly became too time consuming to maintain in parallel, so I brought then under one roof with ***kareninglisauthor.com*** and now encourage any visitors that go to those legacy sites to hop over to my author site. It makes cross marketing so much simpler!

How to get your website up and running

This information is aimed at readers who don't yet have a website set up. If that's not you, skip on to the section *'Key elements to include in your website'*.

I'll be the first to admit that I'm pretty green when it comes to the 'back end' of website design and web hosting. For that reason, **I'm going to limit this conversation to WordPress**, which is the platform I use. There are other options you can look at that appear to be simple to set up — such as Wix.com — but they tend to be graphic based rather than text based so potentially more suitable for use by restaurants, art galleries, shops etc. I've also been told that they can be difficult to migrate to a text-centric website such as WordPress at a later date. Beyond this, I'm afraid I've not tried them and am not qualified to compare them with WordPress.

The two types of WordPress site

There are two WordPress options — WordPress.org or WordPress.com.

I'll briefly outline the differences, then go on to explain why I am currently with WordPress.com but may switch to WordPress.org if I find the time.

• • •

WordPress.org vs WordPress.com

WordPress.org

- You 'self-host' your blog or website with your chosen web hosting company, to which you download the free open-source WordPress software.
- You pay your web hosting company for use of their server — then manage your content yourself (or can pay someone else to manage it for you). Monthly plans can start from a dollar or two a month per site or $5.99 a month for multiple sites.
- You have complete freedom to edit your site's code and have full access to your site's database.
- You have full freedom to install custom themes (designs), third party plug-ins that provide sophisticated analytics, and to monetise your site with advertising and sales.
- You have full responsibility for security updates. Site back-ups may be offered depending on plan level, otherwise you manage these with plugins.

WordPress.com

- Your blog or website is hosted by WordPress.com — there's no software to download. So it's pretty much 'click and go'.
- No hosting fee. Instead you choose between a Free, Personal, Premium, Business or eCommerce plan — the paid plans costing $4/£3, $8/£7, $25/£20 or $45/£36 a month respectively per site, at the time of writing, if you pay annually. You then manage your content yourself (or can pay someone else to manage it for you).
- The Free plan includes third party advertising on your site. I wouldn't recommend this. It also includes the subdomain name 'wordpress' in your site's URL. For example, *kareninglis.com* would show as *kareninglis.wordpress.com* in the browser bar.
- With the Personal and Premium plans you have some flexibility to customise your site/add code.
- With the Business and eCommerce plans, third party plug-ins and full customisation are allowed.
- All paid plans allow you to collect payments — with more sophistication of choice the higher the plan.
- WordPress.com takes care of security for all plans, and offers automated back-ups, and one-click restore for Business and eCommerce plans.

Pros and cons of the two WordPress options

You'll find plenty of blog posts about the merits of self-hosting your website using WordPress.org free software over using WordPress.com to host your site. One key argument is that you could lose your content if WordPress.com disappeared overnight. However, it's perfectly possible to export your content as a means of back-up if this concerns you. On the matter of disaster recovery, WordPress.com assures me that they back up all of their sites each day.

Another historical reason for choosing WordPress.org over WordPress.com had been that you couldn't install third party plug-ins and run sophisticated analytics on a WordPress.com site. However, this changed in 2017 when they introduced the Business Plan option, which allows for all of this and almost all of the same plug-ins as WordPress.org.

The above said, it is clearly a lot cheaper to use WordPress.org than WordPress.com and this is generally the recommended route even though there's a bit more work to do at set-up.

Joanna Penn (a UK thriller writer and self-publishing guru) has a great video tutorial on how to set up a WordPress.org site hosted on Bluehost — found at **http://bit.ly/JPWPress**

If this approach looks too daunting, you might consider paying someone to set your self-hosted WordPress site up for you, then take it over from there. Once everything's in place it's easy to learn how to add new posts, edit content and add images etc.

My current website set-up

At the time of writing, my author website, self-publishing website and the legacy book sites are all hosted by

WordPress.com. I chose this route because when I started out I had no budget, only needed one website and was attracted by their 'free' plan (although I later moved to a paid plan due to the advertisements). I also assumed from what I'd read that using WordPress.org would be a steeper learning curve and require me to be more technically savvy, which I gather isn't necessarily true.

Given the cost differences, I have been considering switching to self-hosting with a WordPress.org site for sometime — but I've not yet found the time! Certainly, Joanna Penn's video gives you a good feel for how the back end of WordPress.org works and it's very similar to WordPress.com.

If you opt for WordPress.com

If you decide against self-hosting, then I'd recommend the Personal or Premium Plan with WordPress.com.

Until recently, I had been using their Premium Plan for both my author site **kareninglisauthor.com** and my self-publishing blog **selfpublishingadventures.com** and found these perfectly adequate for my needs. I've *just* switched to the more expensive Business Plan for my author site, as there was an offer on, but I've yet to try the extra features.

Tip: To get a feel for how WordPress works you could sign up for a free WordPress.com plan and create a dummy (private) website.

A couple of WordPress.com hacks

If you end up going with WordPress.com, here are a couple of useful workarounds, should you need them.

How to include a PayPal button with the Personal Plan

Though not listed as a feature, PayPal sales using a simple button can be set up with the WordPress.com Personal Plan. Simply take a screenshot of the PayPal Button then paste it into your WordPress page as an image and link it to the relevant URL link provided in WordPress's PayPal set-up instructions. You can find those instructions by searching 'PayPal' on WordPress.com

How to mix the free plan with your own URL

I strongly recommend upgrading to the Personal Plan, as a minimum, if you're starting out with WordPress.com today. However, if you *really* can't justify the cost then a workaround when promoting your website address on book jackets or in social media is to set up forwarding from your custom domain address. When your readers type in your domain name, it will forward them to your WordPress.com free site. I briefly did this in the very early days, which meant the browser bars on my sites read as :

- 'kareninglisauthor.wordpress.com' for my author site
- 'selfpublishingadventures.wordpress.com' for my blog

I never had any comment about this, and honestly don't think readers notice that the URL where they land is a variation of your domain name. It's the advertisements on free sites that are more likely to result in customer friction.

Key elements to include in your website

Below I list what you need as a bare minimum, along with recommended additions. What's best to include depends on how active you intend to be online. However, if you do nothing else, be sure to make it easy for anyone coming to your site to (i) find and buy your books and (ii) see how to contact you.

Must-have pages

- Welcome / about me page (could be split across two pages if you want to provide an in-depth bio).
- Books page — ideally one per book, to include blurb, a bit about how you came to write it — with images, and links to sales pages.
- Contact page — for parents / teachers / book buyers. *Include a note to ask anyone under age 13 to get a grown-up's permission before contacting you.*

Recommended additional pages/items

- News / Blog page. If you're not planning to post regularly just make this clear on your welcome page.
- School visits — this is where you'll outline what you can offer. You can embellish this over time as you do more visits and your format evolves.
- Signed or (via Ingram Spark) personalised book orders — if you want to offer these — using a simple PayPal option.
- Resources — a one-stop-shop of your free

downloads, such as colouring sheets, posters and puzzles associated with your book/s. Include these on the relevant book's page to start with, then create this page once you have a collection.

- Newsletter sign-up link. *(See Chapter 7, 'Email marketing', for more on this and what to consider if starting a mailing list for children's books.)*
- Social media links — Twitter, FB, Instagram etc, if you are active here. *(Covered later.)*
- Media Kit — to include links to a downloadable bio and high resolution headshot, book information sheets and contact details.

Legally required pages or links

- A cookie banner, to comply with EU/UK data regulations — WordPress provides one as a widget.
- A privacy policy page — to comply with EU/UK Data Protection rules. If in doubt, watch the Self-publishing Formula Podcast on this topic at **selfpublishingformula.com/episode-117** and use their downloadable Privacy Policy template as your starting point. And/or check out Nick Stephenson's podcast with legal opinion at **blog.yourfirst10kreaders.com/gdpr-for-authors** *(These podcasts are from 2018 – post-Brexit the UK has kept the same rules.)*
- A link to your privacy policy in your header, footer or sidebar and on any newsletter sign-up page.

Tips for website layout

Every second counts when a visitor is on your site, and you want to do all you can to dissuade them from clicking away because they're confused or can't see what they need.

I worked on website navigation design for complex UK Government sites for many years, and sat in on countless user-testing sessions to see how easily customers could complete tasks or find what they were looking for.

While an author website is a lot simpler, I would still encourage you to follow these best-practice tips to make it quick and easy for both site visitors and search engines to discover you and your books:

- Keep your navigation design simple, and ideally on one level, so that customers arriving need only one click to get to any given page.

- Use unambiguous menu labels — 'About me' 'Where to buy my books' 'School visits' *'Book Title'* 'Contact' etc.

- Try to include the target age for your book/s as part of the menu label. This will help visitors find relevant books more quickly — and may persuade them to click even if the title doesn't grab them at first sight. It may also encourage them to investigate books they might otherwise have ignored if the age range triggers a reminder about, say, a niece or nephew's birthday coming up. See my author website for this in action.

- Place your newsletter sign-up link in a prominent position — and start with a call to action: 'Sign up for my newsletter' 'Join my readers' club' rather than 'Readers' club' 'Monthly newsletter sign-up'. Visitors are more likely to respond if you tell them what to do!

- Make it easy for visitors to buy your book — whether from Amazon, other online stores, local bookshops or direct from you. On WordPress the side bar (which remains visible on each page) is often a good place for buy links — as well as for your newsletter sign-up link.

Opposite is a snapshot from part of my author website as at April 2021 where you can see all of this in action. (For a clearer view visit **kareninglisauthor.com**)

This isn't the slickest of sites design-wise, but busy parents or teachers can find what they are looking for quickly, and for me that is the priority. If you can match this type of content with a more beautiful design — and there are lots of free and paid-for 'themes' (designs) to choose from within WordPress.com and WordPress.org — then you'll be way ahead of me!

(If when you read this book, what you see on the opposite page doesn't match what you find online, you'll know that I've finally found time to make changes.)

(Visit kareninglisauthor.com for a closer view)

If my list of books becomes too unwieldy to have them all on the top level, I will move them under broader headings such as 'Books for ages 6-8' 'Books for ages 8-12' 'Picture books for 0-5' etc.

4

FIRST MARKETING: START LOCAL

My top piece of advice for marketing your children's book is to start locally and build up your brand — and your confidence — from there. By the time you're ready to do this, you should have in place the following as a minimum:

- a small stock of your self-published book, ordered from KDP, Ingram Spark or your other supplier
- an author website — however simple or sophisticated this may be
- availability of your book to order on Amazon via KDP Print
- availability of your book to order on other online stores, or by bookshops, via Ingram Spark's feed

You may also have social media accounts in place, but these aren't essential at this stage (or at all if it really isn't for you). *See Chapter 6 for social media marketing.*

Approaching local libraries

One of the first things I recommend is to approach your local library to see if they run story time sessions for children and offer to host a free event there. This is a great way to 'test the water' with live events and, since you won't be charging, it won't feel pressurised. Hopefully, the staff will know you already if you previously enquired about finding beta readers for your book. Bear in mind that they may need a couple of months' notice to set an event up, so plant the idea early on when you meet them and go from there.

My first ever event was at our library in Barnes (the London 'village' where I live) and I was terrified that either no one or hordes of people would turn up! In fact, it worked out perfectly. It ended up being me, my younger sister (taking photos from the back), seven children, around seven adults and a few of the library staff. The librarian, with whom I'd struck up a good relationship during the early review phase, even put up flags and provided tea, orange juice and biscuits! You could offer to bring cake, if it's allowed…

To support the event, I created A4 and A5 flyers that I put up at the library and shared with local schools. This is easy to do using the website **Canva.com** and a colour printer.

See Chapter 8, *'Image and editing tools to support your marketing'* to find out more about Canva.

Approaching local bookshops

Many local bookshops are open to supporting local authors if the quality of the book on offer is of a professional level and is a good fit. While they will be able to order your book online, via the Ingram feed if you're with Ingram Spark, most will prefer to take a small amount of stock on consignment (sale or return) to see how sales go.

It goes without saying that it's a good idea to support your local bookshop by giving them custom — hopefully you'll be doing that already. If not, it's not too late to start now so they get to know you and value your support and thus are likely to be more receptive when you approach them with your book.

If your nearest bookshop is a few miles away, I'd strongly recommend visiting in person ahead of time, to get a feel for the shop. Perhaps buy a children's (or other) book and chat with the staff to find out who looks after the buying side. Take along a copy of your book and a **Title Information Sheet**, designed using Canva and including a link to your website — see opposite for what to include and a link to an example. However, don't necessarily plan to use these right away. If the shop is busy, the last thing staff will want is an unplanned sales pitch form an author they've never heard of!

If the buyer isn't there, ask when the quietest time might be to pop back for a chat. At this point you could mention your book and leave your Title Information Sheet. If the buyer is there, play it by ear. If it's busy you could leave the information sheet and/or a copy of the book and offer to drop back at a later date.

TITLE INFORMATION SHEET

This is an A4 sheet, or similar size, designed to introduce and 'sell' your book to book buyers. The key components of your Title Information Sheet should be:

- Book cover image
- Other images from inside the book (optional, if room)
- Publisher name, publication date
- ISBN, page count and RRP
- Target age range
- Topic/genre — highlighting any topical/educational theme likely to encourage sales (if relevant)
- Synopsis/blurb
- Any testimonials
- Author micro bio
- Contact details: website, email, phone

Then one or both of the following:

- Available locally on consignment — terms 40% (or whatever you decide)
- Available to order from UK /XYZ wholesalers [*on the basis that wholesalers can order from Ingram Spark*]

You'll find an example Title Information Sheet in the resources folder — See Chapter 21 for the password.

Supporting your bookshop with local marketing

If the bookshop agrees to take your book, go out of your way to make sales a success:

- Offer to host a story time and signing session if they have a suitable space.
- Support them by putting up flyers locally to let parents / children know that signed copies of your book are available at the shop. I did this when first starting out, making use of notice boards in coffee shops and local newsagents in areas popular with young families — use Canva for design.
- Offer to provide a 'shelf talker' about your book — these are the mini book blurb / review labels encased in plastic that you see hanging off the shelf in many bookshops. I've done this with all of my books locally, and with Waterstones in the early days. Check the dimensions then create using Canva.
- Go out of your way to mention that signed copies of your book are available at XYZ bookshop in any local press releases / articles or other marketing material you produce — including the 'Where to buy my books' page on your author website.

Marketing to bookshops farther afield

Getting into bookshops farther afield is much more challenging than being accepted locally, where you can drop in consignment stock and stay in touch with the booksellers. It also comes with requirements and financial risks around stock orders and returns that you need to understand and weigh up. I cover this much later on in in Chapter 12, *'Getting your book into high street bookshops'* as wider bookshop marketing really is only something to consider when you have an established track record.

Contacting local schools

Local schools offer the perfect opportunity to connect with young readers, sell your books and start to raise the profile of your 'author brand' through word of mouth. That's the good news. The less good news is that you must be prepared to put in a lot of hard work if you want to get a foot (or should that be book?!) inside their doors. They are incredibly busy places and, unless you strike lucky, it can take a lot of time to get a meaningful response about a potential visit. Also, many will have authors booked months ahead of time and — what with school trips, exams, school inspections, sports days and other festivities — organising a visit from an unknown author isn't likely to be a top priority for them.

I say this only to manage expectations — so don't give up. If you plan ahead and are professional and methodical in your approach, you will get there. I can't tell you how many hours I spent in the early days getting the correct contact names, tailoring emails and following up when I didn't hear back only to be told the teacher wasn't available or that they'd get back to me (but they didn't), or to discover the person I had been told to contact had left. It can be very disheartening, but what I've come to realise over the years is that the school and the staff who you will come into contact with are just **busy**! As a result, emails can be overlooked or forgotten about. Schools that I was convinced were actively avoiding me turned out to be delightful when I finally visited them — often a year or two on from when I'd first contacted them.

To this day, there are schools close to where I live that I've not managed to get into, despite several rounds of conversations and emails. I no longer take this personally. I put it down to their being super-busy — or simply booked up with more well-known authors. But I will try them again at some stage.

Schools close to where you grew up

If it's feasible logistically, why not also contact the school you went to as a child? You are likely to find it easier to book a visit here than at many other schools. When I contacted the primary school I went to they were thrilled, and I spent a day seeing classes with my first three books. Next on my to-do list is to try to arrange visits to others in the area — this is feasible as my relatives still live there, which means I can stay overnight and so avoid a potential cost for the school.

Contacting schools — checklist

- Get the name of the literacy coordinator / school librarian from the school's website or via their office.
- Tailor each email, referring to the school by name and to the pupils by gender if the context is right — for example, if your book is loved by girls and you're targeting an all-girls' school you might mention this.
- Mention any local connections — be that around the

story, and / or local bookshops that stock your book, or the fact that you were a pupil at the school.

- Include your book cover thumbnail(s) in the body of your email or at sign-off — to make the message stand out more.
- **Briefly** outline the age groups your books are suitable for and the suggested format of your visit, ie readings with Q&A and / or workshop.
- Attach a '*Name of author* — Books Overview' PDF with a full blurb of each book. Keep to one page per book and try to make the layout engaging. Again, include thumbnails, a couple of interior illustrations if relevant, age range and perhaps a notable review or testimonial. (If you only have one book then call the document '*Name of author — Book Title —* overview' instead.)
- Attach a separate document entitled 'Visit Format' describing how you will run your sessions and session length — or include this in the books overview PDF if you have room. (I talk more about visit format below.)
- Leave any mention of fees to one side until you have spoken with your contact — unless you're able to offer a visit for free (on which more below).

You'll find an example Books Overview sheet in the resources area at ***selfpublishingadventures.com/resources*** *(See Chapter 21 for the password.)*

Over time, you'll be able to update these PDFs as you sell more books and get more reviews. (For example, *The Secret*

Lake was considered for adaptation by Children's BBC TV a few years ago, so I now include that in a section I call 'Interesting to know'.)

Bonus tip — hand delivery

To increase the chances of your message reaching the right person, you could hand deliver a note with a copy of your book/s and the relevant information sheets to your local school/s. One husband and wife author/illustrator team in the north of the UK emailed me a few years ago to say they had set aside a day and driven around to hand deliver to a dozen or so schools in their area, and had received several bookings as a result!

If you try this, I'd recommend offering to donate the books to the school library (even if they don't want an author visit). Provided you can afford to give away a small amount of stock, the worst that can happen is that your book ends up with more young readers' eyes on it — and who knows where word of mouth might lead?

Working with your local bookshop to approach schools

Many bookshops supply stock for author visits to schools in their areas, and/or have an active school visits programme. Once you have a proven track record, you could offer to team up with your local bookshop — with whom, by now, you should be on good terms — to set up visits, and pass all sales through them. Both of you get to benefit, and even though your income from those books sales will be less than at direct school visits (because you will need to supply your books at a discount to the bookshop), they in turn will be helping you widen your reach and build your brand locally. Note: at this stage you should certainly be charging a fee for your visits.

Playgroups and other parent groups

If you have a picture book, you could also approach local playgroups or other parent gatherings to see if they'd like a free session and the chance to buy signed books for the children. If you're already in a group such as the NCT (National Childbirth Trust) — or the equivalent outside the UK — you could even offer to host an event at home. These more informal groups can provide a great opportunity to test and hone your story telling and related activities. What's more, you'll slowly start to spread news about your brand.

Local events/fairs

Look out for school fairs, charity fêtes and other local events where you could take a table and sell your books. The cost of table hire is likely to be low and even if you only sell enough books to break even, you'll be raising your author brand's profile. And if you make a loss, you've still raised your author profile and had a fun day!

In the summer of 2016, our local football sports centre was organising a family fun day based around the 50th anniversary of the World Cup. Immediately, I saw this as an opportunity to promote *Eeek! The Runaway Alien* due to the World Cup connection. That day, the table cost £15 to hire and I took all of my books along (as well as a blow-up green alien to attract attention!). After the cost of the table, I made a profit of around £30 — admittedly not much for a full day's work from 9am- 5pm. However, I got a photo of a famous World Cup commentator, Barry Davies, holding *Eeek!*, which has been priceless for PR and, a few weeks later, a request for a school visit via the mother of a young girl who bought a copy of *The Secret Lake* at the fun day. That turned into a paid whole-school event during World Book Day week eight months later, plus around 50 book sales.

Family-friendly local attractions

If there are local attractions nearby that are frequented by families would they be a good fit for your book? For example, I live close to the London Wetlands Centre in Barnes, which has a huge gift shop centred around birds and wildlife. It also sells Christmas trees in December. After I approached their store manager in 2019, they stocked *The Christmas Tree Wish* in their shop and have since offered to stock *Ferdinand Fox and the Hedgehog*.

Another idea would be garden centres or children's farms/petting zoos close to where you live. Getting your foot in the door by going in and speaking with the buyer/gift store manager is probably easier than trying to approach a national buyer by email or phone. It's worth a try! Just be sure you know what discount off the RRP you will offer them. If you're supplying direct on consignment with author stock, I'd say 40% works as a rule of thumb. Some centres may prefer to order via wholesalers — if you're with Ingram Spark that shouldn't be a problem. If the manager or buyer's not there when you visit, leave a Title Information Sheet (see earlier under local bookshops) or a copy of your book and plan to return when they are.

Local press, magazines or community websites

Local newspapers, magazines and community websites are always on the lookout for timely and engaging stories, so don't be shy if you think you can find an angle to promote your book. You have nothing to lose, aside from the time to look up the contact and draft your press release. If it comes to nothing, you've at least had practice at press release writing and made contacts that might be useful in the future.

Each book and author situation is different so I can't suggest a generic approach — other than to drive home the local side of the story, and include an engaging image alongside your own headshot with a short bio.

Examples of articles I've pitched successfully to local press

THE SECRET LAKE BOOK LAUNCH

On publication of *The Secret Lake* I emailed our local paper *The Richmond and Twickenham Times* a press release announcing the launch, how the story had been partly inspired by a magical woodland in Richmond Park (a local landmark), and the fact that signed copies were stocked in local bookshops, which I listed by name. I also attached a print quality copy of the book's front cover and my headshot set inside a short bio. A week later, they published the story almost word for word, and added a colour photo of the stunning 'Still Pond,' which I had said had inspired both the lake in the story and the book's front cover design. I got similar coverage in our local village magazine.

Ferdinand Fox's Big Sleep — story retold by special needs pupil

Not long after the publication of *Ferdinand Fox's Big Sleep,* I had a school visit booked in. At that visit there was an incredible young boy named Abe who has cerebral palsy and writes using eye gazing technology. (I had been told this in advance of the visit so had copied the PDF of the picture book to a memory key, enabling him to follow the images close up on his laptop during my author talk.)

By the end of the day, Abe had written and illustrated his own fox story, which his teacher had collated into a mini booklet and brought to me as I was signing books. I was bowled over, as you might imagine! That evening it occurred to me that it would make a heart-warming local interest story, so I contacted the child's parents to obtain permission, which they duly gave. The local paper jumped at the idea and arranged a special photo shoot with me, Abe and a group of his classmates all holding up images from *Ferdinand Fox's Big Sleep* and Abe's book. They published the story in the paper and online later that week.

Eeek! / Henry Haynes / Walter Brown / The Tell-Me Tree / The Christmas Tree Wish

For the launch of each of these books I prepared a short article for our local community magazine, *Prospect,* which has a wide and loyal readership and goes to many young families. On each occasion I included a witty headline, a brief plot summary, enough to hook in readers, a thumbnail cover image and, in the case of *The Tell-Me Tree,* a photo of me by the local tree that inspired the story. I also gave a big push on the fact that signed copies were available in the local bookshop. Most articles went in word for word.

For *The Christmas Tree Wish* I sent a press release to a large circulation magazine popular in Marlborough, Wiltshire, close to where my illustrator Anne Swift lives. The news editor subsequently invited us for an interview at a local coffee shop, where she took pictures of us with the book. The launch was featured in the local online magazine in the run-up to Christmas, pointing readers to where it was stocked locally, as well as online.

Visit to my childhood primary school

I'm never one to miss a PR opportunity and, as soon as my visit to my childhood primary school in Hertfordshire was confirmed, I created a press release and contacted the local press there. In this case, I angled the story around the fact that part of the inspiration for *The Secret Lake* had been the freedom I'd had roaming around in the local woods in Mardley Heath with my friends from a young age — only returning home in time for tea. It was this sense of freedom that I wanted to make part of my modern-day adventure as I wrote *The Secret Lake*. Again, the press release was used almost word for word.

• • •

THE SECRET LAKE HITS AMAZON BESTSELLER LISTS

With increasing online sales of *The Secret Lake,* both in the UK and US, I decided it was time to contact our local press again in 2018. *The Richmond and Twickenham Times* ran an article entitled: 'Local author hits Amazon bestseller lists' on an early right-hand page, and the story was picked up by another newspaper in their network. Unfortunately, the journalist got a few of the facts wrong as he tried to cut down the press release, but I'll forgive him!

You'll find an example press release in the online resources folder.

Will local press coverage help you sell more books?

A few, perhaps — but not bucket loads, and not instantly. But this doesn't matter. The coverage you get is just one part of a marketing mix that's aimed at raising awareness of your books and your author profile. If you remain consistent, it will lead to more opportunities in due course.

By way of example, one summer term I was asked to judge a poetry competition at a local school that I'd never visited. I'm pretty sure they had come to know my name through the mix of media coverage I had had over time, perhaps a few other school visits and the resulting word of mouth. There was no payment for that visit — they had no budget at the time — but their head of English booked me for World Book Day the following year. That day I sold a lot of books and received a £350 fee.

More recently, I was asked if I would be prepared to give a couple of workshops for free at a school a few miles away which was raising money for a school library — I was one of several local authors they had contacted. Again, I didn't know them — so local marketing must have played its part. Parents were asked to make donations to the library fund in return for bringing their children to the after-school event. As well as donating some books to the library myself, I sold almost as many as I would have done at a normal school visit. The school raised around £700 from the author events, everyone went home happy, and I raised my profile some more!

5

SCHOOL VISITS

School visit format

There are a number of ways you can approach school visits and you may need to tailor what you offer according a school's needs — some will be looking for author talks and readings while others will be looking specifically for writing workshops.

Tip: only offer what you know you can deliver well. If running a writing workshop isn't something you feel comes naturally, don't try to wing it!

How I typically run my school visits

- Introduction with slides, including where I work, my cat Misty (who is always around when I'm working) and a quick overview of my books. This works well for ages 6 and above. For the very little ones I keep this element very brief.

- Quick Q&A with the children around what they are reading, why they enjoy reading and / or a topic associated with the book I'm introducing. For the younger ones (ages 3-5) where I am introducing my picture books this is limited to asking them about foxes they have seen and I include images of foxes in my slides, as well as a video of a snoozing fox that fell asleep in a friend's garden and looks very much like Ferdinand Fox! The main aim here is to engage with and earn the trust of the children and make them feel relaxed in my presence.

- A reading from the book — punctuated with pauses to ask questions or comment on the story. This is especially important for the very little ones.

- In the case of picture books and chapter books with illustrations I include slides that show each image as I read.

- Wrap up with 10-15 minutes of questions from the children (for ages 6/7 and above). For ages 3-5 the session tends to end after 30 minutes as attention spans are considerably shorter! For ages 8 and above the questions may go on longer.

- For the older ones I also have slides showing them how I work with my illustrator.

- For the little ones I leave links to colouring sheets and 'how to draw a fox' activities.

I also offer curriculum based writing workshops and/or lesson plans. Putting these together required extensive research into the UK National Curriculum and tailoring writing exercises in line with learning goals and outcomes defined there. These took a lot of preparation, but then I never do things by halves!

If you are an illustrator or good with drama / role play there are, of course, many more options for running your sessions, including getting the children to act out elements of your story. A quick search online should throw up more ideas.

Virtual school visits

Format

As already mentioned, my virtual school visits follow an almost identical format to my in-person visits. I was pleasantly surprised once lockdown hit to find how well this worked.

The key to a successful visit is to **mix things up**, by which I mean varying what pupils see on the screen, how you interact with them and making sure you introduce physical objects during your session. During the course of a 30-50 minute virtual visit here's how I vary things:

- I start out on-screen introducing myself, and asking the audience a few general questions to which they can raise their hands online. ('Who has seen a fox?' 'Who likes reading?' etc.) For my picture book audiences, at this stage I also introduce my

Ferdinand Fox and Ed the baby hedgehog furry characters who sit on-screen throughout as part of the audience.

- For ages 6+ I normally follow up with a more specific question. If it's a small remote group all individually at home, I'll normally pick a pupil to answer based on a show of hands in their individual windows. Where pupils are all in the classroom and / or there are too many watching remotely for me to see them all on the screen, I ask the teacher(s) to pick pupils to answer. Once they start to talk, their window comes into view even if it was offscreen previously.

- Next I switch to slide view — making sure pupils can still see me off to the side in my own smaller window as I talk. Zoom makes this happen automatically when you share your screen but not all other platforms do — so be sure to practise with whichever system the school is using ahead of the event. (See below for more tips on using the different platforms.)

- In screenshare mode, either I'll be introducing and reading from one of my picture books — sharing the images from each page on the screen in PowerPoint as I go — or (for the older ones) I'll be presenting my author talk slides, following the in-person format outlined earlier.

- Note that my slides and how I use them are in themselves designed to mix things up. Thus with the little ones I periodically pause to ask pupils to join in with a rhyme or to raise their hands if they like certain foods etc (this works fine online). With the older ones I pause to ask a question here and there — again mostly such that pupils simply raise a hand, but occasionally I will ask the teacher to choose a pupil to answer individually.

- For the older ones I will stop after a certain time and switch back to full screen view either to read an extract from the book — or to take interim questions. I may also at this time 'show' the pupils something relevant to my talk — eg a proof copy of a foreign language version of one of my print books, the paper manuscript or illustrations with notes and edits, or some other object that relates to what we're talking about.

- I'll then move back to further slides — which normally include a short video (a hedgehog running down the road by my family home for the little ones, and a video of my illustrator drawing *Eeek!* for the older ones).

- We then end up with the final Q&A with me back on the main screen.

- **Q&A Tip:** When I'm presenting to large groups online, I find it works best to ask teachers to gather children's questions in advance and then choose whose will be asked. That way they can ensure a good spread of questions and inclusion of pupils from all the different classes / sites attending. (Where pupils have the same questions they often pick one to ask but cite all names that had that question — this helps more of the children feel involved.) As belt and braces you can also ask the teacher to email you the questions in advance, just in case of sound issues — which can happen! This allows you to take over and lead with the questions if necessary.

Technology for live virtual visits

For security and safeguarding reasons, you will need to use the technology used by the school you are visiting — so be prepared for a bit of a learning curve. Happily, the principles for the main platforms are very similar so once you know one you at least know what to look for in the others — such as gallery view, how to screenshare, chat functions and so on. Less happily, some are far more user-friendly and intuitive to use than others. During 2020-2021 I have so far used the platforms below — and I'm ranking them in order of 'ease of use' just by way of a heads-up!

- Zoom
- Cisco Webex
- Google Meets (via Google in the Classroom)
- Microsoft Teams

How these platforms work is outside the scope of this book but there is plenty out there to help you, so visit their websites and look at their tutorials — and have a dry run ahead of any visit, ideally with your contact at the school you'll be visiting.

In particular find out how to:

- Share your screen
- Switch between presenter view and screensharing
- Get feedback with a poll (can be useful to mix things up when presenting to pupils who are scattered remotely — and easy to do with Zoom)
- View chat, if you plan to use this
- Use 'gallery view' to be able to see all or some of your viewers while you are presenting — including when screensharing. This is simple to implement with Zoom (and Webex, from recollection from the one time I used it), but more complicated with Teams and Google Meets, and may require a second screen if you don't have a large main screen. Or you may have to settle for not being able to see the pupils while presenting — in this case be sure to practise switching back and forth from presenter view and screensharing ahead of the event!

Housekeeping tips for virtual visits

- **Check your lighting ahead of time.** If you have a Mac use the Photo Booth app or start a Zoom / other platform meeting with yourself to test. I have a ring light to one side that provides various temperatures of light that work well at different times of day. Avoid a bright light source behind you, eg daytime window, as you'll appear as a dark silhouette.

- **Make sure your background looks tidy and appropriate!** I tend to arrange my children's books and related promotional images on boards behind me on tables/shelves to add interest and fun. If this isn't possible, you *could* use a virtual background, but I've sometimes seen this cause strange blobby effects so would tend to avoid. A safer alternative would be to erect a temporary screen behind you if needs be — eg using a piece of plain coloured material hung from points off-screen.
- **Check the positioning of on-screen props** — are they in view? You will only know this by testing. Ferdinand Fox sits beside me on a box when I present to little ones but it took a bit of adjusting to make sure he was visible.
- **Have other props to hand**. You don't want to be getting up to find what you need part way through your session!
- **Check your audio and microphone ahead of time**. This should be part of your early research into how to use the platform you will be using.
- **Get the mobile phone number of your contact**. Agree that this will be your back-up should anything go wrong. During a virtual visit on World Book Day 2021 the Internet in our area went down for five minutes — the first time in over a year! Luckily I had the teacher's mobile phone so was able to text her to

explain. Of course, you can email too but I'm not sure a teacher would think to look at their email while managing an online author visit. Happily, things came back up quickly and I was able to log back in.

Pre-recorded virtual school visits

For World Book Day Week 2021 a couple of schools asked if I would provide pre-recorded virtual visits, due to safeguarding issues around live visits. Whilst I knew this would be a lot of work (and it really was!), I was more than happy to make this happen as it had been on my 'to-do' list for wider marketing purposes for 2021 and beyond. I talk more about the tech side of things below.

As with my live author visits, I mixed things up for the prerecorded sessions, sharing my slides at appropriate points with me still visible in a small window at the side. For the readings of *Ferdinand Fox* using PowerPoint images (this approach is needed for picture books I'd say), I found a way to drag that little screen of me and make it larger than the default, to give pupils a clearer view of me. For the readings from my chapter books, which only have the occasional image, I instead stayed in presenter mode and held up poster size images at the appropriate time, rather than flipping to slide view. To see an example of this in action with *Eeek! The Runaway Alien* visit my YouTube channel *'Karen Inglis Children's Author'* then find the playlist for *Eeek!*

While there is clearly no opportunity for live interaction with the children in pre-recorded sessions, I have still gone out of my way to weave in moments where I give the audience the opportunity to respond. Thus for the little ones I still say, *'Put your hand up if you've seen a fox!' [I then pause...] 'Now, of course I can't see you but I bet there are lots of raised hands!'*

I apply similar principles for the talks for older year groups — for example *'Put your hand up if you think it would be exciting to go back in time and meet the children who lived in your house, street or town 100 years ago.'* One thing you could also do here (if the pre-recorded visit is to be shown in class) is to suggest in the recording that the teacher may wish to pause the video to allow children to share their answers/experience in relation to the question just asked. This would be for the teacher to choose to implement or save for later.

Technology for pre-recorded visits

I had a few false starts in choosing which technology to use but in the end opted for Zoom, where I had a meeting with myself that I recorded. Zoom then saves this as an MP4 file that you can check and edit before upload to YouTube. Here you publish it via an 'unlisted' link, which you share with the school. You can later remove or change that link.

I used *Wondershare Filmora 9* to edit the video final file before upload — but you can do this directly in YouTube too (with some limitations). You could also use *iMovie* which is free with Mac — I have iMovie but find Filmora somehow simpler. *Audacity* is another video editing tool, and is free to download.

How to edit video is outside the scope of this book (and I only know the basics in any event!) but it's not that difficult once you know how. You'll mainly need to cut out mistakes or hesitations and check the sound. My advice is to read around, then play around and see what works best for you. It's not an impossible learning curve — you just need time and determination.

- **Recording Tip:** If you make a mistake, just pause for a few seconds or clap your hands close to the microphone, then carry on. When you come to edit the video, you will see the pause as a long flat line on the audio part of the file — or the sound wave spike if you clapped your hand. Move to that section and play it, to make sure you have the correct part, then cut out the error. (It's similar to editing text.)

School visit fees

With so many school budget cutbacks the question of fees for author visits is a delicate one. My short reply to this is that you should request a fee as a rule, but that for your first few visits — while 'cutting your teeth' so to speak — you could offer to visit for free on the understanding that you can offer your books for sale on the day. In many ways this will also put you at ease if you're nervous about how you'll perform.

Talking money is always awkward, but it has to be done! Your offer of the free visit could be couched in terms of your awareness of limited budgets — or, perhaps, that you're able to offer free visits to schools within your immediate area.

(You can slowly withdraw from this 'local free visits' strategy over time once you've established a routine and format that you and the schools are happy with.)

If you are offering free visits temporarily, mention this in your initial email — don't wait until later on. It could make the difference between whether or not you get bookings with schools that are struggling with budgets.

How much should you charge?

At the time of writing, the going rate for author visits in the UK (according to The Society of Authors) is anywhere between £450 and £1,000 per day, depending on how in demand an author is.

However, anecdotally, I know that many authors charge less. Come what may, most self-published authors are not household names, so you will clearly be looking at the lower end of this recommended range — to start with at least.

For in-person visits I currently charge anywhere between £400 and £550 a day. My fee varies according to the size of the school/intake per session, how far I have to travel (time is money) and the school's own budget. It may also be influenced by how many books I expect to sell, though that can be hard to predict.

Most state schools will struggle with higher fees and I'm mindful of this when assessing what to charge.

• • •

My fee range (2021)

- Full day £400 - £550
- Half day morning (three sessions) £250 - £350
- Half day afternoon (two sessions) £200 - £275
- Single session (only viable locally) £85 - £125 or £150 during World Book Day week when demand is high

All of the above exclude travel costs — though I only charge for petrol for visits more than half an hour's drive away. I would also charge for overnight stays, though I have been able to save schools money on some occasions by staying with friends who happened to live nearby.

Bonus tip — school visit cost sharing

If you're invited to or are offering an author visit at a school that will require an overnight stay, ask for — or research — the names of other schools in the area that might like a visit. That way travel and accommodation costs can be shared. For example, back in 2018, I had a request to visit a school in Hereford, which is a four-hour drive each way. I asked if there was a nearby school that might also like a visit and they put me in touch.

It was quick and easy for me to send the second school my information and I ended up with two whole-school visits set up on consecutive days. This is one of the times I was able to stay with a good friend who lived within a 20-minute drive. Needless to say, the schools were very grateful for the saving on accommodation costs!

School visit book orders

To fail to plan is to plan to fail. You'll be on a tight turnaround during most school visits — especially if you're seeing more than one year group. What I hadn't factored in with my first school visit was the time it takes for children to queue up to buy a book and have it dedicated to them. Also, because I hadn't asked the school to collect orders in advance, on the day there were lots of children wanting a copy of *The Secret Lake* but who had no money with them, despite advance notice of my visit being sent out.

In order to maximise sales and minimise tears here's how I now plan for visits:

- Once the visit is agreed in principle I mention that I will supply book order slips in advance to go out to parents
- I ask the school to send these out a couple of weeks before my visit with a return date of 3-5 days ahead of the visit date
- I then ask the school office to email me a list of names/orders to enable me to sign and dedicate the books in advance and top up stock if necessary
- At the same time, I supply posters (made with Canva) for the school to put up to remind teachers/parents/pupils about my visit and the deadline for returning order slips

In some cases the school office checks and collates the cheques/cash for me; in others they simply collect the envelopes and I deal with them after the visit.

You'll find an example book information sheet with order slip at ***selfpublishingadventures.com/resources*** *(See Chapter 21 for the password.)*

What about direct payments online?

At the time of writing I've not used online orders for school visits, but I am looking into it for 2021. I'd really like to cut out the time I normally spend collating individual payments at or after in-person events.

The service/system I choose will be based on how easy it is to set up and, of course, cost.

The main option I'm looking at is a **Payhip** store where I would simply collect payments for books ordered online then match those orders to a list the schools sends me using my tried-and-tested method for all previous visits. This means supplying 'order confirmation' slips instead of 'book order' slips for parents to complete.

Order confirmation slips for schools

For now I am planning a draft order form that includes:

- A placeholder for the web address of my online Payhip store (once it's up!)
- Ticks boxes to indicate which book(s) they have ordered online

- Space to provide the name of the child / children for dedication against the relevant book(s)
- A space to add their online payment reference (the email address used for the order seems the obvious choice here)
- A message to reassure that the email address will not be shared or used for marketing

I will put this experimental order form — and information about the service I finally settle on — in the resources folder once it's finalised. As I am still researching options, I don't want this to hold up publication of this edition.

Other options

My early research has also thrown up **Jotform.com** (US based but says that it can be used around the world). The site is clearly used by many schools for a variety of tasks, and has online order forms with text boxes that customers could use to add names for dedication. It also has templates that can be easily adapted to include book cover thumbnails and — crucially — these forms will integrate to PayPal and other payment platforms.

As I have said, I'm still in research mode but do check them out, especially if you're in the US. There is a free plan, but once you move beyond a certain number of forms and orders you have to pay (on top of the fee your payment processor takes), so it might not make financial sense. If you have a found a solution that works well for online schools' orders, do let me know!

• • •

How many books can you expect to sell?

A very good question! The answer is that it varies hugely and depends on a combination of the following:

- whether the school emails your visit information and order slips, or sends them home in print — print produces much better results as many parents seem to miss the emails and in some cases there is no printer at home
- how engaged the school and class teachers are about reminding parents about your visit and the slip return deadline — a reminder in the school assembly a few days before really helps
- whether or not you supply an eye-catching reminder
- whether and where they put up your reminder poster!
- the demographic of the families at the school — for some there simply won't be the budget to buy your book

As you can see, much of this is out of your hands — so it really is down to trying to establish a friendly relationship with your contact and gently reminding them to remind teachers/parents about your visit as the time approaches.

BONUS TIP: SPECIAL OFFERS/BOOK BUNDLING

If you have more than one book, one tip that can increase sales is to offer bundles. For example, at some schools where I feel budgets may be tight I offer *The Secret Lake, Eeek! The*

Runaway Alien and *Walter Brown and the Magician's Hat* in the following bundles:

- £6.99 each (RRP)
- Two different books for £12 (same family order)
- Three different books for £16 (same family order)

As and when my RRPs change I'll need to revisit these bundle offers, but you get the idea.

If you only have one title you could reduce the price by, say, a dollar or pound to incentivise sales. What you decide to do in each case may vary, and will often depend on the fee you are charging for your visit and the profile of the intake at the school.

6

SOCIAL MEDIA MARKETING

For writers of YA and adult fiction, having a presence on social media offers a great way to connect directly with existing readers and find new ones.

With children's authors it's different as our key audience — our readers — aren't (meant to be) on these platforms. On the one hand this is very frustrating — wouldn't it be great to think that children were reading our posts? On the other hand it is what it is, so look at it positively and make the most of the fact that it *is* possible to target and connect with children's book buyers and influencers directly — something that wouldn't have been possible 10 years ago.

Your target audience on social media will be:

- parents
- children's book bloggers
- teachers / schools
- libraries / librarians

- book clubs
- booksellers / book shops
- clubs / societies / organisations with a theme in common with your book
- other children's authors — *authors can help each other out by sharing and liking each other's posts, getting to know each other and running joint promotions*
- agents — if you're looking for a traditional deal

Visibility on social media platforms — a quick note

Before looking at how to make the most of social media as a children's author I think it important to add the caveat that organic (ie not paid-for) visibility *on all social platforms* has drastically diminished in recent years as the providers seek to cover their costs through paid advertising. In practice this means that only a small percentage of your followers (especially on Facebook and Twitter) are likely to see your various posts unless you pay to 'boost' or promote them. This can be done for a fixed or daily fee that can be as little as $5 and allows you to target just your existing followers or reach a wider audience based on interest and other factors. I cover this later in Chapter 13 *'Children's book advertising'*.

I shall leave further talk of the above until the advertising chapter. Just be aware when reading the next few sections that your posts will not be seen by everyone that follows your social media account — and that 'comment' is your friend! This isn't to say there's no reason to create content — far from it. Some will see it and some will share it if you make it engaging. And if your content is of an 'evergreen' nature, later down the line you can use it as part of a controlled paid marketing strategy if you so wish.

Your only other option is to do nothing at all and I wouldn't recommend this!

Key social media platforms to consider

I'd recommend one or more of those below. You don't need to do them all — better to start off with just one or two and see which you enjoy using the most. You can always add more later.

- **Facebook** — by creating a Facebook Page*
- **Twitter**
- **Instagram**
- **Pinterest**
- **YouTube** — for later down the line**

Facebook*

Note that a Facebook page is classed as a 'business page' — you can't promote your content from your personal page, but do need a personal page in order to set up a Facebook Page. You may also want to create a Facebook Group to encourage discussion and visibility — more on this later.

YouTube**

I'd keep this for later in your marketing strategy unless you are already adept at making videos — it's the one place young readers are known to hang out but will take time to master and you've enough to do already!

You could consider **LinkedIn** but I don't think it's heavily frequented by our target audience of parents who are in 'children's book buying mode'. I'd say LinkedIn is more suitable for raising brand awareness in the non-fiction self-publishing space, or for connecting with illustrators and other professionals.

I shan't go into detail on how to set these accounts up — there's plenty of information out there already to guide you. I talk more about how you can use these accounts below. However, hopefully it goes without saying that you should not flood your timelines with 'buy my book' posts. Rather tell your followers about what you've been up to, share free material or fun images relating to your book, or interesting information from other people that relates to children's books or literacy. Also, be ready to comment on and share engaging content that you find.

How to find and engage with your social media audiences

Clearly your first step is to track down people on the different social media accounts who are having conversations around children's books and fit the profiles listed earlier. Not surprisingly, search is the best place to start. Search using keywords or #hashtags in the browser or search bar on the relevant social media platform. Obvious keywords, #hashtags or search queries might include:

- Children's books / children's book clubs / literacy / middle grade / picture books etc — to identify parents / teachers / librarians who are talking about these topics.

- Homeschooling — to identify homeschool parents.
- Teaching resources / primary teaching / Key Stage 1 and other education-related keywords for your country — to identify teachers of children in your book's target age range.
- Facebook Pages or Facebook Groups dedicated to an author or book in a similar genre to yours — eg Harry Potter, Diary of a Wimpy Kid or Enid Blyton — enter your search term then look at results under Groups as well as in the main timeline.
- Pinterest Boards — enter search terms as above and see what comes up. (Be ready to go down a rabbit hole!)
- On Twitter or Instagram look under #literacy #teaching #childrensbooks #reading #parenting #librarian #primaryteaching etc — to identify accounts you might follow. Also look at people already following those accounts who you may wish to follow.

Creating and finding content to share

As well as commenting on and sharing other people's content you need to have something to say yourself — be that written / visual or a combination of the two. Here are some practical tips to get you going:

- Plan and start to create engaging **written content** around your writing process / book inspiration/school visits/being a children's author and around children's books or book events more generally — in short anything you think your target audience will enjoy and find relevant. I've added full list of suggestions a little further on.

- Make a schedule to start posting your articles to your website or blog.

- Anything you post above can be shared on your Facebook Page, Twitter or Pinterest timeline — and of course those who click will be linked back to your website.

- Plan and create **visual content** to post on Instagram. This can be photos or short video clips. See my Instagram account at @kareninglis_childrensbooks for ideas — and take a look at other authors' accounts there. Anything you post to Instagram is fair game for Twitter, Pinterest and your Facebook page too. Taking pictures is so quick and easy that you'll find that much of this you can do 'on the fly' as ideas or situations present themselves. Don't overdo it though — Instagram accounts that stream endless images in a row irritate me and I suspect others too. I like to see variety in my timeline there.

- Save links to other people's relevant content to share later, on relevant platforms. However, don't just save/share an article blindly because others have — make sure it has something interesting to say and isn't just a sales pitch. Also try to stay mostly on topic (children's books and literacy if you're targeting parents, teachers etc). If you want to share the odd article of interest to self-publishing authors I'd keep those to Twitter / LinkedIn / Google+ as these platforms feel more appropriate for mixing things up a bit.

- Using the groups / people you found during your research phase, follow and engage with those that feel a good fit by liking, sharing, saving and / or commenting on their posts, hopefully to encourage them to follow you at some stage.

- Start posting your own content and links to others' content on your Twitter timeline / Facebook page / Instagram / Pinterest page.

If you do this consistently and naturally — and continue to add to your own blog or website content — you will slowly start to build followers. Depending on what social media you're using, some of your target audience may decide just to follow your timeline there. Others may decide also to follow your blog or join your mailing list. All choices are fine — and it won't happen overnight.

Bonus tips

For the best results bear the following tips in mind.

- Don't be tempted to buy followers or agree to follow others in return for liking each other's pages unless (last scenario only) it's someone whose content you genuinely find relevant. My experience and all the anecdotal evidence is that organic growth of followers will bring you the best rewards and the most loyal engagers. Better a small highly engaged following than a bloated unresponsive one.

- When posting on Facebook always include a photo or a short video as these increase engagement. Ditto for Twitter, though I wouldn't necessarily add a photo every time here. (Instagram, Pinterest and YouTube posts are, of course, image and / or video based by default.)

- Always include images in your blog or website posts — to help break up the text and draw the reader in.

- Break the text into manageable size paragraphs and use bullet points.

- Use keywords in sub-headings and body text to improve discoverability through search — but only do so naturally.

Examples of written content or images you might share

Here are a few ideas of what news and photos / videos you might share:

- how your writing week is going — with perhaps a shot of your office / desk

- school visits or signing events you've attended (take care to get permission from the school or ensure that children's faces are obscured or children are only seen from the back)
- the view from your writing room today
- illustrations from an existing or new book
- excerpts of work in progress
- news or reviews of other great children's books
- links to free downloadable content such as crosswords or quizzes connected with your book or with children's stories in general
- links to lesson plans connected with your book
- links to articles around children's literacy
- photos of letters or creative writing pieces received from readers or school children (ensure any identifying information is hidden)
- screenshots of a nice review you received
- info about children's writing competitions that parents may wish to share
- news about award wins by children's authors
- pictures of your cat or other pet in and around your writing desk or books
- book piles ready for a school signing
- your stand at a local fair/event
- an image of your book in a relevant or famous setting — just for fun
- as above — but with a short video; on receiving my proof copy, I took the new front cover of *The Secret Lake* for a video walk around Isabella Plantation in Richmond Park — the place that inspired the image on the cover and part of the setting for the story

- a short video of your illustrator at work if they can provide this — or of you creating sketches if you also illustrate
- a short video of you checking your online proof or uploading your files to your self-publishing dashboard — I use *ScreenFlow* (paid) to record my desktop
- photo / video of you opening a box of your newly printed book
- Photos sent by parent / teacher of children with your book — but be sure to get permission first
- Photos of virtual author visits — again get permission. Also I'd blur out any children's names that may be showing on their Zoom / other screens

Make this type of content at least 80% of your feed; then occasionally post a promotional post about your own book, or share news about an offer you may have going on.

Remember: Take time to comment on and share others' posts to encourage reciprocal engagement and therefore increased visibility.

Which social media platform is best for children's authors?

The answer is it's likely to be the one that you're most active on. So think hard about which you feel most comfortable using and concentrate on that to start with at least.

The above said, taking into account the children's book buying demographics I covered in Chapter 2, **Pinterest** and **Instagram** are both very strong candidates as places to have a presence because they are frequented by women, who we know are the main buyers of children's books. Out of these two Instagram is the easiest to use and understand, although I'd say Pinterest holds the most long-term marketing potential. I look briefly at how the key platforms work in the following sections. Feel free to skip on if you're already experienced in any given area.

Pinterest and children's book marketing

Pinterest is most definitely worth looking into as part of your social media marketing strategy for these reasons:

- Over 80% of visitors are female — as are over half children's book buyers.
- It's essentially a search engine where people are looking to find a solution to their needs.
- Research has shown that Pinterest visitors are typically in a 'shopping' frame of mind when visiting the platform.
- Your 'pins' (the images you post with comments — and which you can link back to your website or a book sales page elsewhere) will remain searchable if you tag them properly. This means they will have an extremely long shelf life, unlike posts to Facebook, Twitter and Instagram, which are here one moment and gone the next.

Getting started with Pinterest

It can be confusing to start with — so here's a quick overview:

- You set up a profile page with a link to your author website and include keywords in your description that make you discoverable to your target audience when they use search — 'children's books' being an obvious one.

- From here you set up 'boards' grouped by theme where you 'pin' (meaning share or post) images that are relevant to the subject matter of your board. These pins can link back to the source page for the image — such as your blog post — or to another page you choose.

Some boards can be a narrow focus and directly related to you and your work, eg:

- a board for each of your books — including images, book extract snippets, reviews and relevant articles/crosswords — with links to your chosen page, be this a blog post, download landing page of resources on your site or a sales page on Amazon

- a board about your daily writing life

- a board relating to your school visits (taking care not to share images with children's faces without authorisation) — perhaps linking back to a relevant blog post

- a board of free teaching resources that relate to your books with download links

Some of your boards can also have a wider 'theme' focus — eg 'Beautiful children's book covers' — either using 'repins' from other Pinterest boards or images you've found elsewhere on the internet or in your own photo collection. You can also set up 'group boards' along the lines of above but where you allow others to post with your permission. By the same token, you can search for and ask to join relevant boards and pin images you've found there. These can include your own book images, but you'll need to respect the rules of the board and avoid spamming.

Bonus tips

- Join with a business account and link to ('claim') your author website — if you already have a personal account, ask to change it to a business one. Having this combination means others can pin and share your content from your site (and you get access to analytics about this). It also means you're set up for advertising should you wish to do this later on (covered in Chapter 13).
- While you're at it 'claim' and link your YouTube and Instagram accounts if you have these — for the same reasons as above.
- Keep in mind Search Engine Optimisation (SEO)

when naming boards and descriptions — include relevant keywords or hashtags to make your content more findable. However, note that hashtags are no longer clickable in Pinterest as they once were; they act more like keywords. Also, don't overdo them: 4-6 is probably enough — reading around it seems they are considered spammy by Pinterest users, unlike on Instagram where the full complement of 30 is considered acceptable.

- Make sure your pins are optimised to the recommended size — at the time of writing this is portrait with an aspect ratio of 2 x 3 and an optimal size of 1000 x 1500 pixels. Others will work, but you may get quality warnings on smaller sizes such as 600 x 900. Maybe reserve the smaller size images for your website (to prevent slow loading) then use the optimal size for your Pinterest posts.

Long-tail organic marketing

The key point to remember is that it's a long-tail game. If you post little and often, and re-pin and save from boards dedicated to children's books and literacy it will help parents, teachers and others in your target audience to find you and your books. Provided you remain authentic, over time this should lead to more book sales if you have a great book and are targeting the right people.

I dabbled with Pinterest in the early days then ignored it until the last couple of years — more fool me, given that children's book marketing has historically been so challenging!

Pinterest advertising

As with other social media platforms you can choose to promote your pins as part of a paid advertising strategy. I cover my experience of Pinterest advertising in Chapter 13.

PINTEREST RESOURCES

- **IndiekidlitPodcast.com — Episode 34 with Pip Reid** — search online
- **Self-publishing Formula Podcast — Episode 121 with Pip Reid** — search online
- **janefriedman.com/pinterest-market-childrens-books** — a great interview with Darcy Pattison, a US-based children's author

Instagram and children's book marketing

Note: *My Instagram following isn't huge — and this is a direct reflection of the fact that I don't post as often as I should and I don't do 'follow for follow'.*

Nevertheless, influencers have shared posts about my books and I often get tagged by parents/teachers who have shared content about my books.

Compared with Pinterest, Instagram is quick and easy to understand and set up — and with a smart phone you can take snaps and post them right away. **At the time of writing** the available types of post/content include:

- **Posts** — images or short video clips that appear in your main feed; if someone visits your profile they will see these in chronological order with the latest first. Square images work best though landscape will post.

- **Stories** — vertical format — a way to share moments or experiences via photos or video that disappear after 24 hours; normally animated with free add-on gif stickers, text, boomerang effect for videos and / or sound, lasting up to 7 seconds for photos or 15 seconds for videos. (If you run over, Instagram will split your video into up to four 15-second stories — beyond 60 seconds the remaining video is lost.) **Stories don't appear in your feed** — rather they are accessed via your profile button on your Instagram page, which glows with a red outline whenever you've posted a new story. If you want to save a story permanently you can pin it as a 'highlight' to feature above your feed.

- **Reels** — multi-clip videos of up to 30 seconds that **appear in your feed**, made in the moment with the help of a delayed timer, or uploaded from your video gallery — the reels feature offers easy-to-use text, filters and audio clips that you can layer on.

- **IGTV longer form videos** of up to 10 minutes (or 60 minutes if you have more than 10,000 followers)

- **Highlights** — a place to 'pin' access to previous

posts from above across the top of your feed, grouped and labelled by your chosen theme (eg books, events, illustrations, fan mail, readings) — look across authors' profiles to see this in action

Getting started with Instagram

1. Set up with a business account so that in the bio you can include a clickable link to your website, a landing page or sales page — the instructions to do this are easy to follow. The reason you need to do this is you can't add links to your posts until you have 10,000 followers (though there are a couple of ways around this, which I cover later).

2. Use a profile name that lets people know you're an author, such as @yournameauthor or @yournamebooks

3. When posting, refer readers to the link in your posts by including a call to action, such as 'See link in bio' / 'Follow the link in my bio to find out more' etc. (I talk more about making the most of this link in the Bonus Tips below.)

4. When you post an image, include **relevant hashtags** that revolve around children's books, eg:

#ChildrensBooks
#PictureBook
#KidLit
#KidsBooks
#BoardBooks
#EarlyReaders
#chapterbooks

Mix these with hashtags that are relevant or related to the specific theme / genre of your book or post.

This could even include related titles, eg:

#timetravel
#aliens
#magic
#adventure
#fantasy
#enidblyton
#harrypotter
#thesecretgarden

And platform specific hashtags in the mix, eg:

#childrensbooksofinstagram
#bookstagram
#bookstagrammer
#kidsbookstagrammer

5. Widen your reach by adding **broader hashtags alongside those above** — eg based on a location, emotion, time of year, or phrase / saying that relates to your post, such as #feelinghappy #backtoschool #luckymum #summerishere #londonlife. I wouldn't let these wider hashtags dominate the mix but a few thrown in could gain you some new followers or fans, or encourage existing followers to engage with you more — and engagement is all good for the Insta algorithms.

6. Follow and engage with children's book buyers and influencers (book reviewers, librarians, teachers, children's book bloggers) — search under relevant hashtags for each and follow any that look a good fit.

For bloggers a good place to start is **https://blog.feedspot.com/childrens_book_instagram_influencers/** or search online for similar listings.

7. Once you've been following and engaging for a while, if you have a book or new release that you think **is a good fit**, you could reach out to ask if the influencer would like a reading copy for consideration, to share with their followers if they enjoy. These are busy people so don't be surprised if you don't hear back. But if you don't try you'll never know. See bonus tips below for when to be notified when influencers post.

8. Also, see who is following these influencers (this may include parents, librarians, home schoolers) and follow any that look relevant and repeat as for point 6.

BONUS TIPS

- To make the most of your single bio link, send users either to a simple landing page on your site with a list of further links to buy pages or other key content, or use the free plan on the **LinkTree** or **campsite.bio** apps to provide a clean list of links directly behind your Instagram profile. Opposite is a screenshot from my LinkTree page on Instagram. The beauty of these is that you can update and move the links around quickly and easily. You can also embed images, icons or video links. Find out more at **https://linktr.ee/** or **https://campsite.bio/**

LinkTree: you can also add images, icons & video links.

- To get a notification as soon as an influencer you're following posts, go to one of their existing posts then tap the three dots in the top right corner of their screen and choose the option 'Turn on notifications'. Being early with replies to notifications may play in your favour.

- If someone tags you in their post, you can share that post in your story by tapping the paper airplane icon, then choose 'Add **post** to your **story**. (You can do the same to share your own posts as a story.)

- As at February 2021, **anyone can add a clickable link to videos you add via Instagram's IGTV**

button or app. If you have fewer than 10,000 followers, these videos can be between 60 seconds and 10 minutes long.

- IGTV posts don't appear in feeds as I write, but if you create a Story post (text, or mini video up to 30 seconds long) you can introduce the IGTV video and invite followers to 'swipe up' from your story to view it — where in turn you will have included a clickable link.

- In the longer IGTV video you could read an extract from a new book — or even share a full picture book reading. Then promote that reading via a story that points to it — and even promote that story via a related post which of course appears in your feed.

- Taking things one step further, you could turn the story into a 'highlight' which means it will sit permanently across the top of your feed for future visitors to your profile. Search online for **'link an IG story to IGTV with links'** to find out more. While this sounds extremely convoluted, I expect the customer journey is water off a duck's back for seasoned Instagram customers, so if your content is relevant it's worth a try!

Of course, the question is whether any of the above will lead to more book sales — and you'll need to look at the stats for that.

However, remember, if you get clicks but no evidence of more sales, it still all counts towards your brand awareness.

Instagram resources

While these aren't specific to children's books, they nevertheless offer a good insights into how to make the most of Instagram to support your marketing.

- **Self-publishing formula episode -143:** — How To Reach Readers Through Instagram — with Bex Gorsuch
- **Self-publishing formula episode 192** — How to build an audience on Instagram — with Stuart Grant
- **Self-publishing formula episode 252** — How to Get Organic Growth on Instagram, with Hannah Sandvig

Instagram advertising

You can boost posts and run Instagram advertising. This is really something for later in your marketing strategy after other options, and I touch on this in Chapter 13, *'Children's book advertising'*.

Facebook and children's book marketing

Getting started with Facebook

You can't promote your children's books from your personal Facebook page — instead you must set up a separate business page, called a **Facebook page**. However, you do need to have a personal account and page to start with. It's then quick and easy to set up the separate Facebook page.

As a rule I'd call it *yournameauthor* or similar. Other than in exceptional circumstances, I don't recommend setting up a separate page for each of your books. I've been there and done that in the early days and it's just too much to keep tabs on.

Moreover, you want to be able to cross promote all your books in one place. I also don't recommend naming your page after your imprint — readers will be looking for you by name and using it for your page is all part of spreading brand awareness. (If you later run ads, your page name will show as the promoter and will get huge exposure!)

The visibility challenge

I rarely use my personal Facebook page but I do use my Facebook author page (my business page) to try to engage with parents, grandparents, book buyers and teachers and others who have followed me there over the years.

However, like everyone else, I'm up against the fact that most of them don't see what I put up! In my experience, how often your posts are seen organically (ie without having to pay for a boosted post) is connected with who has previously engaged with you on your page and how often. In other words, regular engagers — commenters and sharers — are more likely to see your new posts, albeit the numbers aren't guaranteed.

So, if Facebook is your preferred social media platform, post regularly from the outset and do everything you can to create eye-catching content, ideally with an image or video attached, that's designed to generate likes or comments, or to encourage readers to click a link to find out more.

Also, be prepared to boost your posts from time to time. I periodically pay to 'boost' a new or evergreen post. You can do this for as little as a few pounds/dollars and it's certainly worth a try if you're not getting much traction. You can choose to target your boosted posts to existing followers and/or to new audiences that you can define (eg parents of children aged 8-12 etc). After doing so, you can then invite anyone not already a follower who likes your post to 'like' your page. This not only increases your following, but also means that later down the line you have a larger pool from which to create 'lookalike audiences' if you use Facebook advertising.

Note that you stand to get more sales, if this is your aim, from Facebook ads than from boosted posts. This is because customers can click from your Facebook ad image directly to your sales page, whereas with boosts the photo simply enlarges and you need to place any link separately in the text. I don't think this means you *shouldn't* boost posts from time to time, but understand that the main reason to do so is for brand and audience building, as described above. I talk more about Facebook advertising below and in Chapter 13.

Comments and Facebook Groups as a workaround

As already mentioned, one way around the visibility challenge is through comment and this works both ways. If you leave a comment on someone else's post (say, a librarian's) then it will be seen by the person you reply to, and by others in that thread. This could lead to new followers for you. You will probably also see more posts from that person in your Facebook timeline assuming you are following them.

In addition, many authors are now setting up Facebook Groups where they can chat with fans and followers. For children's authors this is yet another tall order as our true fans are not online! However, if your children's book lends itself to (say) curriculum-related school workshops then, who knows, perhaps a Facebook Group on how best to run sessions based on your book might not go amiss? You could even offer to run a Facebook Live reading for the children there. Provided they are with a teacher in the classroom I see no reason why this couldn't work.

Facebook advertising

As I said above, beyond the occasional boosted post you also have the option to run Facebook ads. Personally, I would only recommend this if you are already making good money from your books and have budget to spare — or you have a strong series that is at least breaking even, or perhaps a non-fiction book in a specialised niche.

Facebook spends money fast, and I've only met a few children's authors who've made it work for them. There are more cost-efficient options when starting out, which I cover in Chapter 13, *'Children's book advertising'*.

I also expand in that section on how and when Facebook ads may work for you.

Twitter and children's book marketing

Twitter, as with Instagram, is quick and easy to set up and understand and offers a great way to share your content.

While in the early days I used Twitter to try to get the attention of parents and book bloggers, Instagram appears to be more popular with those audiences these days. However, Twitter *is* a place where teachers, schools and librarians like to gather. Thus I now focus on seeking out and following these accounts (via hashtags such as #KS1 #primaryteaching #primaryschools #schoollibrarian #edchat etc), taking time to like and/or comment on or share relevant posts from time to time — and I always comment and retweet if any of these audiences tweets about my books. After following, I'll often find I've been followed back.

As part of your strategy to attract the attention of these audiences, be sure also to include relevant hashtags that they may be searching under when you post your own (very interesting!) tweets — eg #readingforpleasure #literacymatters #keystageone etc

See this as a long-term strategy. Don't expect to gain hordes of followers overnight — or indeed at all —fewer quality followers is far better than 100s who may never read your tweets. If your feed is genuine and relevant some of these accounts will, over time, take an interest in what you're doing. In turn, depending on what you are posting, this may lead to likes, retweets, use of your book in class — or even requests for school visits. If you don't try you'll never know!

• • •

Getting started with Twitter

For anyone reading who may not have used Twitter, follow earlier advice for choosing your Twitter name (or 'handle' as it's called) and use the opportunity to add links in your bio to your website/latest book or any other page you wish to market. You can change these links as often as you wish.

A 'tweet' is typically one of the following:

- A short amount of text — ideally with an image attached — with a link to your blog post or other page you want readers to visit, or (occasionally) your book's Amazon page.
- An image accompanied by your comment but no other link (for example a picture of a great book cover you've found).
- A 'retweet' (share) of someone else's tweet by hitting the retweet double arrows icon found in the footer of their tweet. In this case that person's tweet and profile show up in your followers' timeline unaltered.
- A retweet with comment (as above but you add a comment above). In this case your profile appears above the original tweeter's profile in your followers' timeline.
- A repurpose of someone else's tweet, but adapted in order to keep only you and your 'brand' in your followers' timeline. You do this by creating a new tweet then copying the other person's tweet into it, making any edits you want to their lead-in text, then including "by @nameofperson" or similar in

your text, so they know you have shared their content.

You can also respond to people's tweets by leaving friendly or helpful comments.

Twitter best practices

As with the other platforms, follow the 80/20 rule — in other words don't flood your timeline with promotional tweets about your books. Put yourself in your customers' shoes and share content — your own and from others — that you think they would find useful.

Use hashtags to help widen your reach. Users will often use search to find relevant content. See the earlier Instagram section for ideas for hashtags for children's authors.

Thank anyone who takes the time to share your content or information about your books — and use the opportunity where you can to retweet their comments/photos and throw in further relevant hashtags to help widen potential reach.

Twitter visibility

Again, like elsewhere, visibility has become an issue on Twitter as they curate what they show your followers and try to drive more users to boost posts through paid advertising. To improve organic reach, post, comment and retweet regularly and consistently.

I used Canva to design the image in the tweet screenshot overleaf. See my twitter feed at @kareninglis for a close-up and more examples of hashtags I use.

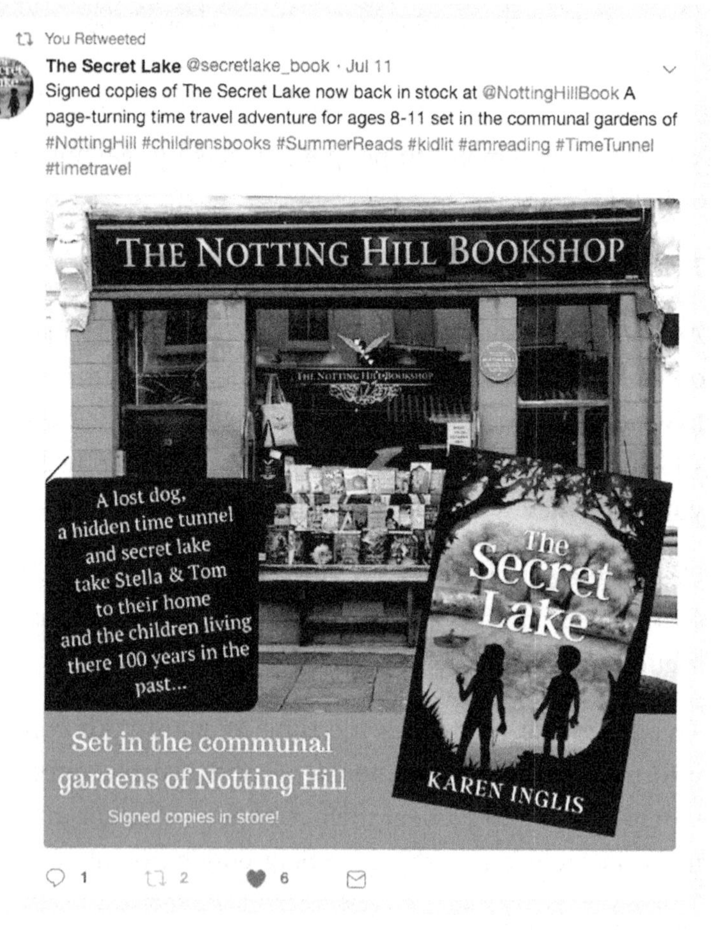

This tweet collage was created with Canva — free software

(There were two parked cars in this photo that I took, so I used text box elements within Canva to mask them!)

Twitter advertising

The general consensus at the time of writing is that Twitter is not a good place to try to sell books — and even then this would be a late runner in any marketing plan. The team at Self-publishing Formula have tested it extensively and had poor results even with adult books. If anything changes I'll keep you updated via my newsletter.

YouTube and children's book marketing

I've had a YouTube channel for many years and had often wondered if it had been worth the trouble of setting up. Then along came 2020 and lockdown when the whole marketing world went virtual. Having everything in place made it easy to pivot and start sharing links to talks and readings I had there already. I also had a place to share pre-recorded author talks for schools that had specifically requested these rather than a live event. (See Chapter 5 for more on this.) I was also grateful that 18 months or so earlier, during a quiet period, I had gone back in and organised my playlists into logical groupings by book title.

The detail of how to set up a YouTube channel is beyond the scope of this book, but the instructions are clear and easy to follow. Pick a time when you're not overwhelmed with other marketing stuff — and be ready to dedicate a few sessions to getting it right. No one needs to know you're doing this until your channel is ready to announce, so don't rush it! Here are a few tips to get you started.

TIPS TO GET YOU STARTED WITH YOUTUBE

- Use your author name for your channel or (if it's taken) a variation of it such as **yournameauthor, yournamechildrensbooks** — anyone searching for you on YouTube is likely to be doing so by name

- If, like me, you have different standalone books, ultimately plan to create a different playlist for each one to make it easier for visitors to find what they're looking for.

- Be sure to tag all of your videos (or, better still, your whole channel) as 'Made for Kids' — this is a legal requirement under the Children's Online Privacy Protection Act (COPPA) and various other children's privacy laws, to prevent data collection from minors and serving personalised ads with your videos. It also prevents anyone from leaving comments (which would potentially expose their contact details), and makes it more likely that your videos will appear alongside others also made for kids

- Use **Canva** to create your header — see Chapter 8 for more details

Video topics ideas

- Readings
- Talking about the inspiration for your book — including photos/video clips from relevant settings
- Interview with your illustrator
- Your illustrator at work / you at work if you're the illustrator
- A tour of your office / work space
- Video collages combining your book's blurb with images from the book — see my YouTube channel

for examples of these for *Henry Haynes and the Great Escape* and *Walter Brown and the Magician's Hat*
- Video collages of letters or illustrations sent by school children
- Book cover reveal / opening boxes of new books / foreign editions

What about live readings?

I've not done any live readings. I just don't have the courage, in case no one turns up! But this is possible using your WebCam — search online for full details, including how to practise via a private or unlisted setting first. You'll need to verify your YouTube account first which is quick and easy. (It is also possible to do via your mobile, but your channel needs 1,000 followers for this option.)

Note: You can't combine livestream with Q&A with Made for Kids videos, as live chat would not be available. On this basis a Zoom visit with a school or Book Club is a better option for Q&A.

You'll find my YouTube channel at **bit.ly/KarenInglisYT** or search Karen Inglis Children's author YouTube.

Video recording software

See Chapter 8 for details of the software I've used to create my YouTube videos.

7

EMAIL MARKETING

How effective are mailing lists for children's authors?

The honest answer is that I'm not sure, and I see very mixed reports from other children's authors in the UK, the US and Australia. I suspect it depends on:

- how you got those readers in the first place
- how much effort you put into creating engaging content
- how well you segment your lists — clearly parents/grandparents and teachers will be looking for different content from you
- how often you keep in touch with your subscribers
- the theme of your books (I suspect that books dealing with, say, children's self-esteem or bullying may see more engagement from mailing lists than straight adventure stories — but I may be wrong!)
- the age of the child(ren) whose parents signed up —

the younger the child, the longer that parent may remain a relevant subscriber if you write across a range of age groups.

I can't say I've had any measurable success with newsletters I've sent out to those on my mailing list, but perhaps if I blogged and emailed more regularly I would find otherwise. My gut feeling is that parents (who I assume make up most of my list) are on the whole too busy bringing up the family to stop and engage with newsletter emails from children's authors — unless they have a genuine super fan in the house.

This doesn't mean it's not worth having a sign-up page though — MailChimp (on which more below) will let you collect up to 2,000 names on their free plan. You have nothing to lose by letting your list grow slowly over time via a sign-up link on your author website and inside your books. At the very least it gives you the opportunity to let people who've enjoyed your work know when you have a new title coming out, or have a title on offer. I certainly saw a sales spike for *The Secret Lake* around the time I emailed my list when the new cover came out, even though I hadn't been in touch for many months.

Keeping subscribers 'warm'

To be the most effective, however, you need to keep your subscribers 'warm' in between times with occasional updates about what you've been doing — perhaps with new links to free resources such as crosswords or colouring sheets associated with your book that you know they've not had before. I have to confess that with my other tasks of writing, briefing my illustrator, organising school visits and other promotions I've mostly found myself somehow out of time when it comes to email campaigns. But that doesn't stop you being more active!

Volume vs quality of email sign-ups

The growth in organic subscribers from my website and back-of-book sign-up pages has been very gradual — just a few each month. The only large jump I've had was after running two Giveaway promotions in collaboration with other children's authors where we each emailed our own mailing list with a combined offer. (*See Chapter 10 for more on Giveaways.*) In one I gave away an eBook copy of *Eeek! The Runaway Alien* and in another I offered the first three chapters of *The Secret Lake* for free. However, engagement from those subscribers was negligible in the follow-up emails I sent, and I've heard other children's authors say the same.

My conclusion is that sign-ups when promoting a free book via a mass promotion gives a poorer quality of subscriber than those you get through your own efforts — perhaps because many may never get around to opening your book as they already have Kindles stuffed full of freebies.

To try to improve the quality of subscribers you get in any joint promotions I'd recommend requiring double opt-in to your newsletter (meaning after they tick the box to sign up, they have to reconfirm their subscription in an email that gets sent to them — this is best practice though not mandatory).

Email sign-ups and EU/UK data protection law

Note that when wording email sign-up copy with a Giveaway, it's important to stay within the EU's General Data Protection law, and the UK's equivalent rules. These state that consent to provide personal data must not be made a condition of being able to receive a product or service. This applies for any sign-up sequence that you send to customers living in EU / UK countries, and is especially relevant if you are offering a Giveaway or discounted book to help build your mailing list. In short, pre-ticked boxes for newsletter sign-ups are not allowed — customers must be able to opt out of the data collection process and still request the freebie. And if they do sign up, they must be able to cancel any future promotions or newsletter subscriptions.

Personally, I would apply this for all customers worldwide — logic says that those who **choose** to join your list will be good quality leads; those who don't join may still read your book and, if they enjoy it, might yet come back for more.

Whichever route you decide, let your subscribers know roughly how often you'll be in touch then plan accordingly.

(I talk later in this chapter about how to ensure your sign-up wording complies with rules around data protection for children.)

A moving target

Keep in mind that your subscribers' children are growing all the time — so what might have been of interest for them 18 months ago is no longer of interest today. A clever way to try to manage this might be with a sign-up questionnaire asking children's ages in your first email back — but how likely parents/grandparents are to respond is another question. If you give it a go, do let me know how you get on!

Targeting grandparents

Trying to collect emails of grandparents separately through targeted lead generation advertising, or a separate email sign-up link on your website for grandparents, could prove a fruitful strategy. I think it's a safe to say that grandparents are likely to have more free time than parents — and many will have disposable income that they're dying to spend on the grandchildren. Targeting grandparents has been on my never-ending to-do list for some time and is something you may wish to consider.

Targeting teachers and librarians

It's also possible that teachers (including home-educators) and librarians could provide you with a better 'return' on your invested time than parents. Thus you might want to consider having a separate sign-up for this group on your website — clearly marked as so. Email broadcasts you send here would have a different nuance than those for parents, and you may find better engagement. I have various curriculum-based teaching plans for my children's books that I offer as workshops at school visits and it's been on my to-do list for some time to find a way to promote these to teachers in return for an email address. It will undoubtedly take time to build up lists such as these and — as with social media marketing — you'll need to (a) create content that you can share with them regularly or semi-regularly (b) earn their trust and interest by engaging with them in the places they hang out online.

2021 Update — segmented email sign-up

I have finally found the time (just!) to create a separate sign-up for teachers/librarians for 2021 — long after I had suggested this back in the first edition of this book in 2018! Clearly, it's too soon to say how well this this will work but I'll provide updates via my self-publishing newsletter.

Creating street teams from your email list

Many authors of YA/adult books use segmentation to create 'street teams' of superfans of their books who have indicated they would be interested to beta read early drafts, and leave reviews at launch. Busy parents may struggle to find the time, unless it's a picture book, but this could work with teachers, librarians or grandparents. Why not give it a go?

Newsletter sign-up: best practice for children's authors

As children's authors we need to take extra care not to flout the rules around data protection for minors. Yes, we are keen to communicate with our young readers but the law rightly says we cannot market to them directly, and that if minors are contacting us it must be with the express permission of a grown-up. For that reason I would recommend including a form of words along the lines of *"If you're under age 13, please ask a grown-up to sign up for you"* when composing sign-up pages (children on your site may be tempted by your free download offers).

The screenshots below show how I put this into practice. They also show how I keep to EU/UK marketing rules by making it clear that they are signing up for my newsletter — the free downloads are a bonus 'thank you'.

Sign up to my newsletter

Sign up to my readers' club occasional newsletter below. As a welcome I'll send you a ***free eBook preview of The Secret Lake***, my bestselling time travel adventure for ages 8-11 to share with your children. (Also perfect to read aloud to ages 6 and above.)

I don't email often and will never share your email address. Unsubscribe at any time. Privacy policy

YES PLEASE - SIGN ME UP!

Step 1 — This clearly address the message to parents.

Sign up for my readers' club

Please enter your details below. *(Important: if you are under age 13 please ask a grown-up to sign up for you.)*

FIRST NAME

EMAIL ADDRESS

SUBSCRIBE

Step 2 — Here I clarify the minimum age for sign-up.

Choosing a mailing list service

A good place to start out is MailChimp, which is free for your first 2,000 subscribers ('contacts'), subject to certain limitations.

Alternatively, look at ConvertKit, which has a free plan for up to 1,000 subscribers — again with certain limitations.

I currently use Convertkit's $29 a month paid plan for my author website followers, and Mailchimp's free plan for my self-publishing followers. ConvertKit is not the cheapest option once you have to pay but, in my view, has a simpler and more logical user interface than Mailchimp. It would therefore be my recommended choice if you find you need to move beyond a free plan. Time is money and, in my experience, it's worth paying the extra for the time saved not going around in circles inside MailChimp!

Another option is MailerLite, which I've heard is very good value, though I've no experience of using them.

Find out more at:

- **MailChimp.com**
- **ConvertKit.com**
- **MailerLite.com**

Mailing list sign-up pages — hosting options

If you use WordPress.com's Premium Plan or above — **provided you are using their block editor** (which I assume is the default for newer subscribers), you can host email sign-up pages for MailChimp and MailerLite directly on your WordPress site. This won't work if you're using their older Classic editor — as I am. In addition, at the time of writing, integration is not available for ConvertKit, with or without the block editor.

In case this affects you, not being able to host these pages on your website isn't a problem — my sign-up links take readers to a page hosted by my provider (ConvertKit) for my author website, and to a page hosted by MailChimp for my self-publishing blog. The customer journey here is seamless and doesn't affect my ability to gather subscribers. See below for an example sign-up landing page hosted on ConvertKit.

My WordPress.com sign-up links go to ConvertKit hosted landing pages

I can't speak for other sites' rules on hosting sign-up pages I'm afraid but the information should be easy to find.

How to encourage email sign-ups

In the early days of my author website I simply asked for sign-ups in return for occasional news about upcoming events, new books and special offers. I got a few but not many. Today you need to be more imaginative and offer something in return. *Reminder: under EU/UK Law you can't* ***require*** *newsletter sign-up 'in return' for any of these.*

Here are a few ideas:

- The first chapter or two from your bestselling book in eBook or PDF format.
- A short story you've written that's not available anywhere else in eBook or PDF format.
- Links to illustrations from inside your book.
- A downloadable colour poster of one of your book covers.
- Colouring sheets using images from your picture book.
- A quiz, word search or crossword puzzle relating to one of your books.
- A free audiobook or early chapters from an audiobook in MP3 format.
- For teachers: links to class activities, teaching plans or audio or video talks related to your book.

I recommend ***BookFunnel*** for delivery of eBooks, PDFs and audiobooks. I cover this in Chapter 11, *'Tips and tools for sending out eBooks'*.

8

IMAGE AND EDITING TOOLS TO SUPPORT YOUR MARKETING

Canva: for image marketing and flyers

Much of your content and brand marketing will rely on images — either to attract readers to your online posts, or in the form of flyers or posters to help promote a school visit, other event or book release. You will also need images of a set size to use as headers in your Facebook and Twitter profiles, or — later down the line — to run Facebook or other online ads.

Happily, most of the images you need for this come free — in the form of your own photos or artwork/illustrations from your book, to which you own the rights.

A tool that I highly recommend for adapting these to support your marketing is **Canva**. This is free to use, with an optional paid upgrade. I finally upgraded to the paid version in 2020 and it does offer extra bells and whistles including more design options, stock photos and animation options. However, the free version is *more than enough* for your needs if budgets are limited.

At **Canva.com** you can create:

- posters and flyers to promote your school visits or other live events
- correctly sized headers for Facebook, Twitter, Instagram and other social media platforms
- Facebook and other ads to the correct size
- correctly sized photos or image collages for social media posts on Twitter, Pinterest, Instagram or Facebook
- and more…

The tweet collage image in Chapter 6, with *The Secret Lake* at the Notting Hill Bookshop, was designed with Canva.

What I particularly love about Canva is **how easy it is to use** — just like Vellum its user interface is uncluttered and intuitive and it makes image editing a truly joyful experience! It's also quick and easy to update an existing design for re-use, as I explain below.

School visits reminder poster

I have a poster that I send to schools ahead of my visit, which they put up to remind parents and pupils about my visit date and the deadline for returning order forms. For each new event I simply pop back to Canva and update the visit dates and deadlines, tailor any other text as necessary then hit 'download' and email the PDF to the schools. It really takes all of five minutes. Just a few years ago this would have required back and forth emails with my illustrator — and the associated cost — as I didn't have access to Photoshop or any other layering software.

Find out more at **Canva.com**

Reminder poster designed with Canva

Bookbrush: 3D covers and instant mock-ups

Another tool that I highly recommend is ***Bookbrush.*** Designed specifically for authors, it allows you to create ads, social media posts and other promotional material for your books at a click of a button using 3-D mockups for eBook, print book and/or audio format. (For each of these formats there is a range of templates to choose from and you simply drop in your book cover.)

For background, you can upload your own photos or access over a million royalty-free backgrounds to which you can add text, fade out and other filters, as well as book-related buy buttons and stickers. As well as using this 'Custom Creator' function to design your ads, you can choose from a range of pre-designed templates searchable by genre, including children's books.

There are four plans — Free, Plus, Gold and Platinum — none of which is prohibitive. If your budget will stretch to it, I'd recommend the Gold Plan ($12.25 a month/$99 a year at the time of writing), which also offers 'Instant Mockups' that allow you to drop your book cover into ready-made scenes with real people reading your book. The instant mock-up that follows (which is in colour in real life, of course) was created on ***Bookbrush*** in a matter of minutes!

Other ***Bookbrush*** features include background video with or without sound, the ability to create box set promos, and book covers for print, eBook or audio.

While the website navigation could use a little improvement, once you know your way around ***Bookbrush*** offers a fantastic addition to your marketing armoury. The great news is that you can 'try before you buy' and register for free without a credit card to test it out. What are you waiting for?!

Bookbrush.com

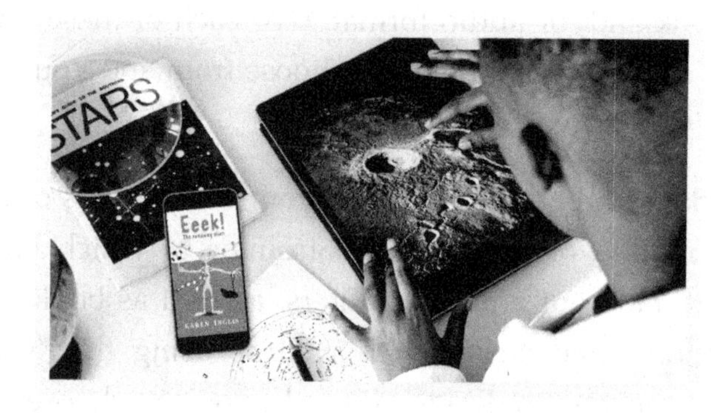

This instant mock-up took three minutes to create!

Video creation and editing software

Further down the line in your social media and content marketing, you may wish to create videos with captions or fun features such as blended scene changes and/or music and sound effects.

Here's what I've used:

- **My iPhone** — to create quick videos to share on my blog and in social media posts — such as my walk around Isabella Plantation in Richmond Park with the new cover of *The Secret Lake* in May 2018.
- **Zoom** — to record myself — using the meeting function. When you end the meeting it saves the file

as an MP3 which you can then edit afterwards (more on this below). Zoom has free or paid plans.

- **YouTube Editor** — to add captions to talking head videos I've uploaded there or to trim/edit videos uploaded from Zoom.
- **iMovie** — part of the free Mac suite — for creating, editing and exporting book trailers to YouTube and my blog, using a collage of images from inside the story then adding music and captions.
- **Wondershare Filmora (paid video editor)** — in preference to iMovie, I now use Wondershare Filmora which I find simpler and more intuitive for creating or editing videos. Indeed, if you google it you'll see it rates highly for usability for all levels, combined with a reasonable cost. At the time of writing it's on offer at a one-time fee ('perpetual licence') of $69.99 down from $79.99 for the basic package, which is what I have. Alternatively you can subscribe monthly for $9.99.

For all of the above, I taught myself by following the instructions and referring to YouTube videos. Anything is possible if you're prepared to put in the time!

Though I've not yet tried it, I believe it is also possible to edit video footage directly inside Facebook. If this is a platform you use a lot it's worth checking out.

If you visit my children's author YouTube channel at **bit.ly/KarenInglisYT** you'll see examples of the book trailer videos I've made. These were all done for free, following the instructions on YouTube and/or iMovie, which comes free with my Mac. The author readings were recorded on Zoom and edited with Filmora.

Finally, below is a March 2021 link to more free or low-cost video editing services. (*Disclaimer: I haven't tested any of the sites.)*

bit.ly/vid_software

9

FIRST REVIEWS: DIRECT REQUESTS

Getting those first reviews is the Holy Grail for all writers and a double challenge for children's authors, as we can't engage with our readers directly to offer review copies. However, it's not impossible, it just takes time — partly because those parents and teachers and other influencers we can engage with have 101 other things on their to-do list, and partly because even once they are on board the children or pupils they will be passing your book on to also have busy lives.

How I got early reviews for my books

1. Using contacts in the book world

In the case of both *The Secret Lake* and *Eeek! The Runaway Alien* I received 5 Stars from the ex Head Reader for Puffin UK who now runs *The Writers' Advice Centre for Children's Books* in London, which I recommend for editorial review if you're in the UK. Ten years earlier I had done a one-day course on writing for children that she had led. I thought she might not remember me when I contacted her — but she did and was more than happy to review my book. If you have contacts in the world of children's literature — or perhaps an English teacher whose review could lend gravitas to your book — why not reach out to them early on to see if they'd be prepared to read and review it?

2. Beta readers

When looking for beta readers for *Walter Brown and the Magician's Hat* at the final draft stage, I offered a free book in return for their feedback once the book came out. When I supplied those books, I enclosed a short thank you note which included the suggestion that they might like to leave a review on Amazon or their other preferred website with a parent's help, as it would help other parents and children find the story. (I found these beta readers via a school I had visited previously. Along with the draft manuscript, I supplied a simple questionnaire for the pupils to complete and their teacher set them 'read and review' work over the October half-term break.) I'm not sure if that led to reviews, as I didn't know the children other than by their first name — but you have nothing to lose by trying this for your next book while it's at final draft stage. And if you know the parents or teachers who passed on your book you could always follow up a few weeks later with a gentle reminder.

3. Early review copies via my local library

The concept of beta readers hadn't really emerged when I wrote *The Secret Lake* — rather I used the services of a professional editor, as recommended above. But as soon as the book was out I offered early review copies via our local library.

From the outset I explained that I'd be looking for parents to help their children leave a review on *The Secret Lake* website (about which more below) and on Amazon if they enjoyed the book. This certainly worked, with several parents posting reviews on behalf of their children on Amazon and children posting with their parents' help to my website. I sent a polite reminder to one or two after a few weeks, but it was in no way 'pushy' and in no way obliged them to leave a review.

4. Reviews on The Secret Lake website

Many of the children who received early reading copies of *The Secret Lake* left reviews with their parents' help on a dedicated page I set up on the book's original website *thesecretlake.com*. I alerted parents to this page, and it's also mentioned at the back of the book. My hook was, and still is, that if children leave a review I will reply to them on there.

At the time of writing the first edition of this book, while the review page was still promoted at the back of *The Secret Lake*, it only received the occasional review every few months, if that. This was a direct reflection of the lower sales of *The Secret Lake* at that time. Most organic reviews (which trickled in VERY slowly compared with those you might expect when selling YA/adult fiction) appeared on Amazon. Thus — to simplify my life —I was on the verge of mothballing *thesecretlake.com* site along with the reviews page. However, around the spring of 2018 after I began advertising on

Amazon UK I suddenly saw sales of the book start to spike. Given the new numbers, I thought it best to hold off mothballing the site and reviews page after all. Lucky I did! Fast forward to today and that page is filled with dozens of new reviews from children all around the world, to whom I always reply! You can view it at *thesecretlake.com/reviews*

In light of the above, while getting Amazon reviews is a priority, you could also set up a review page on your author website where children could leave reviews of any of your books. (I don't advocate creating a separate site for each of your books.) However, bear in mind that you must be extremely careful to follow the strict rules around privacy and data compliance for under 13s. (You will see that my page is dominated by warning messages about who can and can't post there — it's not a pretty sight and probably results in many reviewers clicking away!)

Aside from the priceless direct contact these reviews give you with your readers, they of course offer you a further marketing opportunity as you can include them in ads or social media posts along with an image of the book. Taking it one step further, you can also create a collage of review excerpts in Canva and post these as an image to your preferred social media platform.

5. Contacting Amazon Reviewers

A few weeks after I published *The Secret Lake,* I read on a blog about Amazon's 'Top 500' reviewers on Amazon.com, so I did some research and found the list. Scanning down I quickly found someone who reviews children's books (and other products) but clearly also loves history and historical dramas on the BBC. This felt a perfect fit for my story which is historical fiction, so I emailed to see if she'd like to review it. I was astonished to hear back within the hour — she told me that she wasn't taking on much as she was extremely busy, but so liked the look and sound of the book she'd like to review it. I was then thrilled when she dropped me an email within a week to say that she'd read it to her six-year old daughter and given it five stars! (This was especially heartening as she had explained that she doesn't post reviews unless a book is worthy of four or five stars, but instead lets the author know she felt it didn't work). These reviews are referenced and linked to from my website, and you can of course see them on Amazon.

How to find reviewers on Amazon

Despite my early success above, I'd say the most efficient and targeted approach to finding children's book reviewers on Amazon is to look through the list of reviewers of children's books that are similar to yours then click on their profiles. Some may include their email address or a website which means they are fair game to contact — and are probably open to the offer of review copies. Or you may be able to track them down via their social media account if you have their name but no other contact details. I've done this once or twice — but more by chance when I happened to be reading a review of someone else's book and thought the reviewer seemed a good fit for one of my books.

You could also try the approach I used for *The Secret Lake* of looking through the Top 100 (or even the Top 1,000) Amazon reviewer lists, but this could be very painstaking! I think I was very lucky to find my reviewer — and at that time she was in the Top 10 so I stumbled across her very quickly. From a quick look, the Top 100 Amazon reviewers these days are largely men reviewing gadgets! If you still wanted to try this approach, search for ***'Top 100 Amazon Reviewers'*** in Google and you'll find the relevant pages. If you strike lucky but do not see any contact details, you could, as suggested earlier, try searching for the reviewer on social media platforms if they are showing their first and last names. If they offer a public means of contacting them there, then it's certainly worth a try.

Tip: Research the reviewer lists carefully and **only email reviewers who are a genuine fit for your book**. Don't expect an instant reply, but do follow up after a couple of weeks if you've not heard back. Finally, be aware that Amazon has changed its rules around reader reviews in exchange for a free book, so you and the reviewer will need to take care to comply. I cover this in more detail at the end of this chapter.

Children's book blog reviewers

There are plenty of bloggers who write about and review children's books. Many make money by then using affiliate links out to Amazon, which means they earn a small referral fee from Amazon if readers go on to buy your book.

Below are some good places to start. Read their small print and only approach those that are a genuinely good fit for your title in terms of target age range and genre. If they say they don't accept self-published titles then respect that.

- **Reedsy** — their listing of vetted book review blogs, which is regularly updated, allows you to search by genre (including children's books) and by those that will review self-published books. **blog.reedsy.com/book-review-blogs/**

- **The Federation of Children's Book Group**s — a list of UK children's book review sites broken down into bloggers who accept picture books, middle grade and / or YA, as well as Librarian and Teacher reviewers. (Not all will accept self-published books). **fcbg.org.uk/book-blogs**

- **Book Sirens directory of children's book reviewers** Book Sirens is an ALLi partner member, which means it's been vetted as offering a good service. Access to its directory of reviewers is free and you can sort by bloggers that accept children's books for free or paid reviews. Check out their children's book review page at: **bit.ly/booksirenskids** It certainly looks intuitive and I have seen good feedback from a few children's authors. (Book Sirens can, subject to certain guidelines, manage this process for you. I cover this in the later section on sending out Advance Reader Copies.)

- **Feedspot Reader** — a listing that includes the top 100 children's book bloggers and influencers from around the world based on site activity (from what I can see). **blog.feedspot.com/childrens_book_blogs**

These apart, search Google or Facebook for children's book bloggers.

It can be time consuming identifying bloggers that are a good fit for your book, and even then you may find that they won't be able to guarantee reading/reviewing your book for many weeks or months.

Whatever the quoted turnaround time, it will be worth the wait if the blogger has taken the time to reply to you, and has written quality reviews for books in a similar genre to yours. If they accept eBooks you have little to lose if they end up not reviewing it. However, if they only accept print books (which will be the case for many reviewers), I'd still go ahead in this situation and post them a copy with a nice cover letter.

In the early days of *The Secret Lake* I got a handful of lovely reviews this way, which was a real confidence booster and useful for sharing on social media.

Note: I'd personally be wary of any blog site that asks for a fee in return for fast-tracking your review.

Using KDP Select free days to request reviews

If you have an eBook that's in KDP Select this can be a good way to ask for reviews — not least because, at the time of writing, reviews posted will count as 'verified purchases' by Amazon.

Free Days - Case Studies

Two examples of when KDP Select free days can be especially effective for new book launches are:

If you have built a 'street team' of super fans

These would be readers who have opted in to beta read your early drafts and offer feedback (covered in Chapter 7). As part of this process you let them know when the final book will be going on sale for free for a limited period, which means they are primed to download it and any review they leave will count as verified. Whilst you *cannot require that they leave a review in return* (that is against Amazon's terms), the likelihood is that many will if they joined your street team because they genuinely enjoy your books.

I should caveat this by saying that while this is a tried and tested practice for authors of adult and YA books, it's likely to be harder to make work **in high numbers** for middle grade novels because parents are less likely to have time to take on the commitment of reading a longer children's book. In addition, their children — your target audience — generally prefer to read in print. This isn't to say it won't work — I know that it has for some middle grade authors. It's more to say that it won't be as straightforward as for YA/adult street teams whose members are also your target audience and are used to reading eBooks. Where you may have more luck is if there are teacher and librarian fans in your street team as they probably have a vested interest in reading your book for research purposes. Grandparents with more time on their hands may also be a better bet, as previously mentioned.

If you write picture books

KDP Select Free Days can work well for getting reviews if you write picture books and join Facebook or groups of picture book authors where self-promotion and/or feedback requests are allowed. Many picture book authors are also parents and will be happy to download a free copy of your book and consider leaving an honest review based on their own reading and/or after sharing it with little ones. The beauty of picture books is that they are quick to read — thus the chances of getting willing readers and reviews is high compared with doing the same for chapter books or middle grade novels. Of course, always check whether group rules allow you to post review requests — and join in offering your own feedback and advice on others' posts before diving in with your own request. Many of these groups include requests for feedback on book covers, titles and storyline — it's not just about review requests for KDP free days. Needless to say, you will find yourself on the receiving end of similar requests.

I can't talk from first-hand experience about how effective street teams are for getting early reviews for middle grade novels as I haven't used them. But I have gained — and given — early honest reviews for picture books this way, using the method described above.

I talked more about the pros and cons of being in KDP Select in Chapter 14.

10

SPECIALIST REVIEW / PROMOTION SITES, AND GIVEAWAY PROGRAMMES

These options are, of course, suitable both for seeking early reviews and to help boost reviews for backlist titles. Having a good clutch of (honest) reviews is always helpful if you're running Amazon ads.

Children's book review services

1. Wishing Shelf Reviews

Wishing Shelf Reviews is run by the team behind The Wishing Shelf Book Awards, which works with teachers and schools and has been vetted and recommended as trustworthy by The Alliance of Independent Authors. Their review service complements the awards competition and at the time of writing charges $99 (£79) for a guaranteed, honest and in-depth review of your book from their selected pool of editors, authors and teachers. They will also place reviews on Amazon and Goodreads if you wish. Find out more at **thewsa.co.uk/needareview** (I talk more about The Wishing Shelf Book Awards in Chapter 17.)

2. LoveReading4kidsUK Reviews (UK)

LoveReading is a well respected book recommendation site. It is split between *LoveReading.co.uk* for adults books, *LoveReading4Kids.co.uk* for children's books (each with a large book-loving mailing list) and *LoveReading4Schools.co.uk* – used by teachers, librarians and parents for reading lists.

Here's how it works:

- You submit your title in eBook form.
- A LoveReading Ambassador from their trusted team reads and reviews it within 4 or 8 weeks, depending on which plan you choose.
- Your book's details are also sent to LoveReading's consumer panel of 1,000 reviewers who have the option to review your book after downloading a sample
- If an Ambassador reviews your book well it will be listed on the main LoveReading4Kids and/or LoveReading4Schools site for free.
- A positive ambassador review also results in an "Indie Books We Love" LoveReading4Kids graphic to use on your site/book and enters your book into LoveReading's Indie Book of The Year Competition
- At the time of writing the cost is £120 and 4 weeks' turnaround for a picture book review, or £120 and 8 weeks' turnaround or £170 and 4 weeks' turnaround for other children's books.

This is another option to consider if you're struggling to get reviews and have some budget, not least as a sample would go out to a large panel of potential consumer reviewers, offering a means to spread news of your book through word of mouth as they browse and download samples from the site. Furthermore, assuming your book's landing page on LoveReading will show all reviews (do check this!), it will provide another place to point to, or from which to quote reviews.

Find out more at **lovereading.co.uk/your-book-reviewed**

3. The Children's Book Review (US)

This is a well respected and nicely organised children's books site that offers professional honest reviews, author interviews and featured showcases at different fee entry levels.

In particular, there is an option to showcase your book through the site's free 'Author Showcase Basic' option.

For this you submit a review of your book in your own words along with any images you'd like shown. The editorial team then reviews what you send and reserves the right to edit it as they see fit, include all content as received — or not to include the content at all.

I'd say you have nothing to lose here. If they choose to include your interview it will provide valuable extra online discoverability and a page on a suitable website to point to as part of your social media marketing.

Back in 2011 and 2014 I opted for interviews for *The Secret Lake* and *Ferdinand Fox's Big Sleep* as I had so little presence beyond my own websites online.

At the time of writing, the starting cost for an unbiased and professional paid review of at least 200 words, guaranteed to appear within 4-5 weeks, is $245, with incremental increases for books of over 50 pages.

Whichever option you choose, look at it as one part of your much longer-term marketing plan — it won't necessarily lead to an immediate jump in book sales and it could take a long time to earn back any investment. If budgets are tight, stick with the free listing.

For details of the basic (free) showcase option, visit the link below — you'll find it as the last option on the page: **thechildrensbookreview.com/dedicated-review-submissions/media-kit/author-showcase**

To read about the paid reviews options visit: **thechildrens-bookreview.com/dedicated-review-submissions**

Website: **thechildrensbookreview.com**

4. Toppsta (UK)

Toppsta is a bright and fun website dedicated to children's book reviews **written mostly by children** who have received a free copy of the book in a Toppsta Giveaway. Children sign up via a parent or other adult in order to leave their reviews, and earn points for doing so.

At the time of writing — due to overwhelming demand for its service — it's no longer possible for self-published authors to submit books for a Toppsta Giveaway. However, what you can do (and the owner has confirmed this to me) is **run your own Giveaway** and suggest that children or parents post their reviews on Toppsta as well as on other sites. If your book is on the Ingram feed it should appear on Toppsta, and customers can both review it and order it from there.

Look at Toppsta as just one of many steps in the long-term strategy of raising the profile of your book with a permanent page containing reviews. At the very least, the children or teachers who read the Toppsta reviews will now know about it. It also offers another platform to point towards for reviews from your social media feed, or to lift review excerpts from for inclusion in a Canva collage for use in newsfeeds — with a link back to your book's page on Toppsta. This could be a lifeline if you're struggling to get reviews elsewhere.

See the site at **toppsta.com**

5. Schoolreadinglist.co.uk — Not taking submissions from new contacts at the time of writing but I'll leave it here in case that changes.

The above list isn't exhaustive, but gives you a place to start.

Specialist platforms for seeking reviewers

1. StoryOrigin

StoryOrigin offers a way for authors not only to build mailing lists through 'Giveaways' (on which more later), but also to send free eBook copies to readers who are actively seeking books to review in a particular genre — including children's books.

The site offers an in-depth checklist for how to make the best out of this feature, including how to 'vet' potential readers by checking the quality of their previous reviews before handing over your eBook.

A detailed overview is beyond the scope of this book but it's certainly a site to check out, to see if it could be a fit for you either now or further down the line in your marketing as a way to get reviews. I don't know anyone personally who has used the review feature but have seen good reports about the Giveaways for building mailing lists. Certainly one to check out — I'll be doing the same!

At the time of writing in April 2021 there's a free Basic plan, which you can integrate with your mailing list provider, and a Standard Plan, designed to help you grow your mailing list and get reviews via group promos, newsletter swaps and more. The cost is $10 a month or $100 per year.

StoryOriginapp.com

2. BookSirens

BookSirens — an ALLi partner member — will manage sending out Advance Reader Copies for you if your book meets certain criteria. They offer this service via both their free 'DIY' plan and their paid-for 'Author' or 'Promote' plans.

Acceptance onto their system is at their discretion after you complete a questionnaire. As their reviewers tend to like new books, your title must have a future publication date, or have been published in the last 30-90 days, depending on the plan. You also have to answer key questions about the editorial and formatting process your book has gone through — this is good news as quality is clearly on their radar.

On their free plan (if they accept your title) you can set up a landing page where readers/reviewers can request and download your book. It's up to you to do the promotion of the link. With their paid plans (if they accept your title) they will manage getting reviews for you. With all plans you get to stipulate the maximum number of books that can be downloaded.

Compare their price plans at **bit.ly/BSirensPrices**

BookSirens.com

3. Hiddengems

I've not used Hiddengems but know of some children's authors who have, with mixed results. The site has a huge mailing list of book reviewers who can search by category and sign up to receive a copy of your book in return for posting an honest review on Amazon and any other sites they use. You pay a $20 non-refundable deposit to book dates to be included in their mail-outs. This includes your first 1-10 readers. After that you'll pay $3 per reviewer (up to a maximum of 140 reviewers).

Amazon's rules strictly prohibit paid reviews and Hiddengems states that the fee is to cover the cost of connecting authors with readers and maintaining their site. There is no obligation for reviews to be left, although members who consistently sign up for books and don't review them lose membership over time.

From reading around, the reviewers are known for being brutally honest, so don't look at this as a quick way to get high-starred reviews. I'm including this for completeness as it comes up in discussion quite often and could be of interest at some stage. Just be careful what you wish for!

Find out more at **hiddengemsbooks.com**

EBook Giveaways: solo or joint promotions

Running eBook Giveaways either individually or teaming up with other authors in your genre has been a tried and tested way for authors to increase reviews and/or build their mailing lists over recent years. While on balance I'd say it lends itself best to YA and adult titles (because children's books are normally read in print), it may be worth a try if you're struggling to get reviews. The main players facilitating this at the time of writing are:

- **BookFunnel**
- **StoryOrigin**
- **Prolific Works**

Each works similarly, typically as follows:

- An author announces they will be running a group promo on one of the above sites and invites others in the same genre join in. Authors add their free books to a combined promotional page — titles are normally set free for a given time which is announced as part of the promotion.

- Each author promotes this combined page to their own mailing lists and on social media.

- Customers browse the page and click through to each book's landing page for more information and / or to download it, sometimes in exchange for an email address, sometimes not, depending which plan you're on.

- Prolific Works also run and manage themed Giveaways themselves which you can sign up to, and which they promote to their own mailing lists.

Mailing list integration

BookFunnel and StoryOrigin offer integration with the main mailing list providers including Mailchimp, MailerLite, ConvertKit and more. Prolific Works only integrates with MailChimp and MailerLite at the time of writing.

Ahead of the Giveaway you set up your title's landing page inside your BookFunnel, StoryOrigin, or Prolific Works account. It's from this page that the customer can download your free book, and have the opportunity to sign up to your email list at the same time — depending on which plan you are on. As with ARCs, you have the option to limit the number of downloads per promotion and to set an end date.

Remember: EU and UK GDPR rules say you cannot *require* EU/UK based customers to join your mailing list to get the free copy, thus wording of the offer needs to make this clear for those audiences. As I've said previously, I think you're better off letting all readers make that choice in any event.

In terms of which to choose, I'd say take a look around, read reviews and choose the one you feel most comfortable with. I'd highly recommend BookFunnel for ease of use in delivering eBooks and, having looked through StoryOrigin's features and tutorials and read feedback from other users, would say it ranks up there with BookFunnel.

Do eBook Giveaways really work for children's books?

My admittedly limited experience with a few Prolific Works joint promo Giveaways for ***Eeek!*** back in 2017 was that I got thousands of downloads but very few reviews or extra paid sales in return. This experience is not untypical and, while not limited to children's books, I think we children's authors have an especially hard time making this work for the following reasons:

- The person downloading isn't normally the reader, so we then need to rely on them to pass on the book to their child, and with their busy lives it's inevitable that many won't get around to it. In addition, they then will need to chase the child for a review and help them post it.

- Most children under age 12 prefer to read in print, so the format may be a barrier to many from the outset.

The subscribers I gained through the above group promotional Giveaways have been the least engaged of all on my mailing list and I have since culled many of them. I'm sure that 'free books overload' will have played a role there!

That said, I know this strategy does work for some authors — most notably those who write *in a series* for the higher age range within middle grade (9-12). If that's you, it's certainly worth a try. Moreover, we know that reading habits for children's books shifted towards more eBook reading during the pandemic, so this sort of promotion may prove more fruitful than previously if some of those habits stick.

Using BookFunnel Print codes on flyers or bookmarks at live events as a way to give away eBooks *may* lead to better quality results. I cover this in the next chapter.

Goodreads Giveaways

Goodreads — owned by Amazon but left largely to its own devices — is a website where avid readers from around the globe discuss and swap notes about books, create reading lists, and leave book ratings and reviews. Think global reading club. Any reader who is signed up to Goodreads can leave a review there, so it's worth mentioning it when sending out review copies.

In return for a fee the platform allows you to offer your Kindle eBook or KDP Print book in a Giveaway to help raise its profile and (hopefully) garner reviews.

Note: At the time of writing Kindle Giveaways can only be run to readers based in the US, and print book Giveaways only to readers based in the US or Canada. This is a change from previous years and the site indicates that the options are due to widen again in the future.

How it works

Site visitors coming to the Goodreads' Giveaway page can search by genre and by country in which the Giveaway is available then sign up for their name to go into the draw.

If they sign up your book is automatically added to their 'Want-to-read List' which helps raise your book's profile visually on a site that's visited by thousands of readers every day. Also, any followers you already have on Goodreads, and any readers who have your book on their 'Want-to-read' List already will be notified of the Giveaway.

For print Giveaways you must use KDP author copies to fulfill winner orders, either shipping them directly from Amazon or placing orders for you to sign at home then send on.

Goodreads Giveaways were free to take part in until late 2017 — and weren't limited to the US and Canada as they are now. They proved very useful for me in the early days. I gave away 3-5 print books each time and, in each case, sent a hand signed copy with a card and short note asking if the winner would mind leaving a review online — ideally on both Goodreads and Amazon. This worked well for *The Secret Lake, Ferdinand Fox's Big Sleep* and *Eeek! The Runaway Alien*. However, with *Walter Brown and the Magician's Hat* I had less luck — and by that time was starting to hear stories of people failing to get reviews. There is a perception —

which may or may not be correct — that there are now a lot of people who sign up for Goodreads Giveaways just to get hold of a new book that they can re-sell online.

At the time of writing it costs $119 to run a Giveaway using Goodreads' Standard plan and $599 with the Premium plan. Premium plan extra key features include:

- Your title will feature higher up the Giveaways listing pages, making it more discoverable
- Goodreads will email winners after eight weeks to remind them to rate and review your book — this is good news!
- You can create a customisable message for Goodreads to send to entrants who don't win — giving you a chance to talk directly to hundreds or thousands of readers who have expressed an interest in your book. Note that you can't include URLs or newsletter sign-up requests, but there's nothing to say you can't suggest they search online to find out more about you and your books. (I'd check this though!)

In the case of children's authors, I'd use this as a last resort option and am really only including it here for completeness. If I were writing for adults and in a series I might be tempted to give the Premium Plan a go given the additional features it now offers.

To find out more visit **Goodreads.com** and search 'What are Giveaways?' Also expect more countries to be added (back) in due course.

Advance reader reviews — latest Amazon rules

Note that the rules I mention below may have evolved by the time you read this, so always check online.

In the traditional world publishers have for many years obtained early reviews for new titles by providing ARCs (advance reader copies) to selected readers who are keen reviewers and/or to other authors in a similar genre. ARCs are provided ahead of the official publication date so that by the time the book is released there are already reviews in the press or online — or these quickly appear online soon after launch.

As already described, self-published authors have been using a similar method to get early reviews on Amazon and elsewhere in recent years — and rightly so. This is how the publishing industry has always worked and, provided the reviewer is not required to leave a review, the practice is within Amazon's rules. (As I understand it, it is no longer necessary for the reviewer to say they received a free review copy, though this was once a requirement.)

Alongside this approach, and since Amazon introduced the **'verified purchase'** badge against reviews a few years ago, some authors have offered a time-limited reduced price of the eBook version of a new title to enable advance readers to leave 'verified purchase' reviews soon after launch after buying the book for 99c/99p.

However, in the early summer of 2018 Amazon updated its guidelines to introduce the following restrictions around reviews. As far as I can see this hadn't changed in 2021.

- It is limiting how many 'non-verified purchase' reviews a single reviewer can leave to no more than five in a week.
- It requires reviewers to have spent a minimum of $50/£40 on Amazon on the store in question in the last 12 months.
- Its guidelines also seem to suggest that where a large number of verified reviews appear at a book's launch, some of these may be removed in the interests of transparency if it suspects that an artificially low and short-lived introductory price on an eBook was used solely to get those verified reviews. (This is my interpretation at least.)

I regularly see authors reporting reviews being taken down, or their advance reviewers not being able to post because they have reached their review limit, or for some other unknown reason. Here are a few tips to try to avoid this.

Tips to minimise loss of reviews

- Don't ask family members or close friends to leave reviews — Amazon somehow works this out.
- If sharing links to your book, keep them clean — ie strip them back to the book's 10-digit Amazon identifier number that comes directly after the book title. (The information that comes after this may include data that links the original search back to you. Amazon may then make the assumption that you are sharing the link with a family member or close friend even if that's not the case.)

- Don't try to influence reviewers or **require** them to leave a review in return for a free or discounted copy of your book.
- It may be wise to ask for reviews to be posted elsewhere as well as on Amazon — to avoid the risk of losing them altogether — forewarned is forearmed! Goodreads is the obvious choice here.
- If you have a large reader team or mailing list, you might also want to look at staggering review requests or launch emails to avoid Amazon flagging unusual behaviour on your account and unfairly removing reviews.

The rules may have changed or been further clarified by the time you read this. Either way, if you plan a strategic launch involving a lot of advance reviewers, I'd strongly recommend searching in author forums to check the latest rules and facts.

11

TIPS AND TOOLS FOR SENDING OUT EBOOKS

Send a Word document to Kindle

If you want to supply an eBook copy of your book for review before it's been formatted for Kindle, a quick and easy way to do this is to email the reviewer a Word document to their Kindle address. It will then magically appear ready to read on their device.

For this to work they need to 'allow' their Kindle to accept an email from you. This is easy to set up, but they probably won't know how. Here are some handy instructions that you can send them:

Reader instructions

1. Go to Amazon and log into your account.
2. Click on 'Your Account and Lists' (top right on a desk top) then **either:** from that label's dropdown menu choose 'Manage your content' **or** on the main

page that loads, choose 'Content and Devices' from inside the box entitled 'Digital Content and Devices'

3. Choose the tab / link 'Settings' (it's one of three links towards the top of the page).
4. Scroll down and click on 'Personal document settings' (it's the 7th or so heading about half way down).
5. Under 'Send to Kindle-Email Settings', you will see your Kindle's email address (if you have more than one Kindle there will be more than one email address).
6. Copy the email address for the Kindle you want to read the manuscript on and send it to me once you've completed Step 7.
7. Under 'Approved document email list' click on 'Add new approved email address' and enter my email address which is *[author insert your email address here]*. My email address will now appear in your approved list.
8. Now email me your Kindle's address that you copied at Step 6.

Author action

Email your Word document to the reader's Kindle address in the normal way as an attachment. You don't need to include a subject line, but you can if you wish. The book will appear on their Kindle's home page when they next sync it — with a placeholder cover based on the file name.

Using BookFunnel to deliver eBooks

BookFunnel is a fantastic service that enables authors to send readers free eBooks quickly and seamlessly. If you're planning to share eBooks as part of a launch strategy or a more general Giveaway, or need to send an eBook to a book blogger or other reviewer don't let this pass you by!

Their First-Time Author Plan at $20 per year should more than meet your needs to begin with. Once you're ready to expand your marketing, the Mid-List Plan ($10 a month or $100 a year at the time of writing) is still excellent value.

Here's how their main offering works:

- You create a private landing page on BookFunnel with your book's jacket, description and a download link to your ePub, PDF (— or MP3 for audio).
- Once the landing page is ready you can generate as many separate links to it as you wish for segmented marketing purposes.
- You then set a download limit and / or deadline date then share the landing page link with your mailing list and / or via social media — depending on who and how you are targeting.
- When a reader clicks on the link you sent them, BookFunnel handholds them through choosing the right file format for their eReader and then guides them through how to get the file onto their device.

The above features are available on all BookFunnel Plans. If you're on one of BookFunnel's plans that includes email integration you can alternatively use their 'Certified Mail' feature for ARCs.

With Certified Mail, BookFunnel will:

- send a unique link to each email address on your review team
- track who downloads your book and send automatic reminder emails about the launch date
- watermark the files they provide and expire all links automatically at the end of the campaign

BookFunnel only recommends using Certified Mail with active review teams, to avoid emails otherwise landing in spam folders, and to avoid irritating readers who don't know you well with reminder emails.

You can also use BookFunnel to sell your eBook direct from your site — though read up on the sales tax implications first. I talk about this in Chapter 14 under *'Pros of going wide with your eBook'*.

BookFunnel.com

BookFunnel eBook Print Codes for live events

In 2018 BookFunnel introduced unique, non-sharable Print Codes to use on flyers, bookmarks and other marketing material. These allow you to give away your eBook in person at events, while preventing multiple downloads. Children's authors might use these at local fairs or bookshop/library readings, or in hand-outs after a school visit, for example.

Since providing a unique code on each flyer or bookmark would be costly, as a workaround you could print or hand-write the codes onto white or coloured Avery type labels at home and stick these onto your hand-outs.

Another option would be to have have bookmarks/handouts with a non-unique BookFunnel landing page URL that takes users to a Giveaway page. In this case you would make it clear on the handout that it's a 'first come first served' offer, and set a limit for the number of downloads. There will be no issue with extra print costs for having the link address within the flyer or bookmark because the design won't vary. Or you simply use stickers as above. With this option I'd recommend using one of the link shortening sites such at **bit.ly** to create a reader-friendly URL. You can of course vary the URL by different event.

At the point of download you can give the reader the chance to sign up to your email list if you wish — albeit you'll need to adapt any email sign-up message to ensure that it's the parent and not the child that signs up, as described in Chapter 7 on email marketing.

As the child is in the driving seat in this scenario, it could increase the chances of them reading and reviewing the book (or at least telling their friends about it!) than if their parent had signed up from an online offer.

Their First-Time Author Plan at $20 per year should more than meet your needs to begin with. Once you're ready to expand your marketing, the Mid-List Plan ($10 a month or $100 a year at the time of writing) is still excellent value.

Note that you need to be on BookFunnel's Mid List Plan to be able to create unique codes. However, you can use the workaround with a non-unique URL if you're on their First Time Author Plan.

To find out more, visit **BookFunnel.com**

12

GETTING YOUR BOOK INTO HIGH STREET BOOKSHOPS

I've left this section until late on deliberately, as I don't believe it viable for most self-published authors to achieve many sales across high street bookshops beyond their local or near-local stores. Moreover, trying to get your books widely stocked comes with financial risks.

Barriers and risks around getting into high street bookshops

I shall start with the challenges. However, it's not all bad news! The next section looks at a workaround in the UK that may help if you have a strong track record and know you will be able sell any returned stock if things don't work out.

Barriers

- Unless you have an established sales track record or the backing of a publicist then booksellers are unlikely to order your book, even if you tell them about it. Shelf space is limited and they want to order what they know will sell.

- They also know that readers are unlikely to come looking for your book if you aren't known already, or part of an established publishing house that may be helping raise your profile in the background.
- Most traditional publishers have a national sales team that sells into bookshops at face-to-face visits. With the larger chain stores these sorts of deals are done at a centralised level. Trying to compete with this will be extremely difficult.
- At the time of writing, bookshops' ordering systems typically show print-on-demand titles as having a long delivery time (often a few weeks) even though they are usually printed within 48 hours of the order. This is all down to delays in the supply chain between the printer / distributor, the wholesaler and (in some cases) bookshops' own centralised distribution hubs. Thus, even if a bookshop took an interest, the ordering timeline would throw up an instant barrier — as well as the risk of losing the sale to Amazon while waiting for the order to come in.

Risks

- Most bookshops won't stock a book they can't return — which means you'd need to accept returns and the associated costs. (Of course, if a customer places an order that's a different matter — but see last bullet above.)

- If you were serious about trying to get into multiple stores you'd need to print a lot of stock up front. How would you cope financially if it all got returned?
- You'd either need to pay a substantial amount for sales and publicity support, or spend considerable time and money yourself mailing and/or emailing bookshops to tell them about your book — and ditto for national media to raise your book's profile.
- Historically, publishers have paid the major high street book chains to have their books placed on bookshop tables and/or face out displays. While some booksellers may have moved away from this strategy to one more closely based on what customers want/are buying, they are still more likely to offer these spaces to traditionally published books that are supported by strong marketing budgets as they know that people will come looking for these titles. So, even with all the efforts above, there's a strong risk that very few people will find and buy your book.

In short, trying to get into non-local bookshops only makes sense if you have a strong marketing campaign and/or very strong online sales that have led to word-of-mouth publicity meaning that both readers and booksellers have your title on their radar. Only then might it be worth printing stock up front and taking the risk of allowing returns.

Clays UK printers helping self-publishers and bookshops

The above all said, there is one solution in the UK that gets around part of the problem — using Clays printers to make it quick and easy for bookshops to order your book. This option could make sense if you have evidence of demand and have a back-up plan to sell returned stock if necessary. For example, if you have a book that sells well in schools, this could be your back-up. (Note that Clays doesn't offer full colour printing at the time of writing, so this will not work for picture books.)

How the Clays arrangement works

Clays here in the UK (**clays.co.uk**) — are printers for many traditional publishers, including Nosy Crow and Hodder to name just a couple.

As well as offering digital short runs alongside their offset longer-run printing service for larger clients, Clays also has a great set-up for small and self-publishers to make ordering by high street bookshops easier. In short, they will hold up to 100 of your short-run books in their warehouse and send requested orders to Gardners wholesalers using a special distribution arrangement they have with them.

If you sign up for this service, it means that UK bookshops who use Gardners (by far the majority) will see your book as being 'in stock' on their till's data feed.

As a result, provided they know about your book (and this is where my earlier caveat about marketing campaigns comes in), this gives it a far higher chance of being ordered than if they see it as being on several weeks' delivery, which a print-on-demand title typically shows.

Fees and wholesale discount

Note that this is a specific distribution arrangement that Clays has with Gardners. At the time of writing the key things to know are:

- you need to offer a 50% discount off the RRP of your book to Gardners
- Clays takes 6% of your RRP for each sale
- you receive 44% royalties less the print cost for each book sold

This is not a bad deal by any means. However (to emphasise the point yet again) it really only makes sense if you raise awareness of your book through a concerted sales and/or marketing campaign — and/or if your book is already selling well on Amazon to the extent that word of mouth means customers may start asking for it. If this isn't the case, it's unlikely that either booksellers — or browsing customers in the shops you do manage to get into — will end up noticing and buying your book.

Case study: The Secret Lake with Clays

I've been making *The Secret Lake* available on a returns-allowed basis through the Clays/Gardners arrangement since 2018.

I initially decided to try this for three reasons:

1. *The Secret Lake* had been selling very well since early 2018, gradually creeping up the rankings and appearing in Amazon children's book bestseller lists. (In fact, it reached 75 in the whole of the Amazon UK store at one point in July.) This made me think that those who don't shop on Amazon but began hearing about it through word of mouth might start asking for it in bookshops.
2. I had been due to top up my own stock anyway. Instead of using Lightning Source, I used Clays for an order of 200 which came in cheaper than ordering via Lightning Source. Clays kept 100, of which 30 went to Gardners on an 'allow returns' basis and Clays held on to 70 (no charge) to supply Gardners if they needed more. Clays delivered me the remaining 100 (no delivery cost), which I kept to supply my local bookshop, and for school visits stock.
3. I knew that if things didn't go to plan and the Gardners books were returned, I could sell them at school events — also that the cost of posting returns would not be charged to me.

My profit per sale on the above print run was less than on Amazon by around £1 per book. This was understandable because there was now a wholesaler in the supply chain, which is the only way I can meet UK bookshop demand. However, more book sales means everyone's better off and it's great to be able to support bookshops as well as Amazon!

Fast forward to 2021, and with continued regular sales via Clays I've gradually increased my print runs which has brought down the unit cost and reduced reprint administration time. Thus I went from 200 to 500 and, most recently, to 2,000. This latest order has reduced my cost to around 80p a book, meaning each sale via Gardners now earns me around the same as my Amazon sales and significantly more for any sales I make direct at events.

During this time I've continued to promote *The Secret Lake* not just through Amazon advertising but also on a gradual drip feed basis through social media, newsletters and my website where I make clear that it can be ordered online or through any high street bookshop.

As at end of March 2021 I'd sold over 1,860 copies of The Secret Lake this way. On the back of these sales I've also persuaded Gardners to accept small stocks of my other titles on a no return basis, so if customers ask for them in bookshops they can get them quickly. I'm able to keep an eye on the Gardners' stocks from the public facing page on their website simply by typing in my author name in the search bar. If I see those small stock numbers start to dwindle I call my contact at Gardners to ask if he can order a few more. (NB: I think he allows this because I am selling so many copies of *The Secret Lake* — it took a long time to get here!)

Further essential reading on getting into bookshops

For an in-depth look at getting into bookshops, see ***'Your Book into Bookstores: ALLi's Guide to Print Distribution for Authors'*** by Debbie Young, published by the Alliance of Independent Authors (ALLi).

You can download it for free along with many other useful guides if you're a member of ALLi. *See Chapter 19 for the benefits of joining ALLi.* Otherwise you can buy it online or from the ALLi website.

Also, see the UK's Booksellers Association 2017 handy guide to getting into bookshops. Although it's a few years old, it's still useful. Find it here: **bit.ly/bookshopsguide**

13

CHILDREN'S BOOK ADVERTISING

Below I cover the main options to consider for paid advertising. *Spoiler alert:* Amazon ads is where I recommend you focus your attention and for that reason this is by far the largest section. Once you've been using Amazon ads for a while, try some of the other options *if you wish* then run with what works best for you. Whichever path(s) you choose, **be sure to spend only what you can afford to lose.**

Note that I highly recommend you supplement your reading on Amazon ads with the books I recommend during and at the end of the chapter. They cover more than children's books, but there's lots to learn in them!

This chapter includes:

- Amazon Advertising through KDP
- Facebook and Instagram Ads
- Pinterest Ads
- BookBub Ads — for eBooks only

Note: Some authors, myself included, have access to Amazon Advertising through the Amazon Advantage program as well as via KDP. The program was designed for sellers with physical stock (rather than eBooks or print on demand books), but a few determined self-publishers managed to find a way in before KDP offered ads.

While the Advantage program offers some additional advertising features as I write, I suspect these will all become available on KDP in time. I mention Advantage here in case you see it referenced in forums, or see other ad types running on Amazon. My assumption is that if you are in the Advantage program you already know enough about Amazon ads anyway so I shan't be expanding on it below. As far as I'm aware Advantage is closed to new author applicants.

Amazon Advertising through KDP

Certainly the game-changer for many self-published authors in the last few years, including me, has been the ability to promote our books on Amazon, using Amazon Advertising (previously called 'Amazon Marketing Services' or 'AMS', an acronym you may come across). The service allows you to run ads for your print and eBooks using a variety of ad types, and in a wide range of territories.

As at April 2021 you can set up and run ads from your KDP account in the US, UK, Canada, Australia, Germany, France, Italy and Spain. You set your daily budget, targeting, maximum cost per click and how long you want to run campaigns for — and, crucially, you only pay when a customer clicks on your ad.

In short Amazon has opened up its shop window and digital table space to everyone. It then keeps it stocked based on what customers buy.

A level playing field for self-published books

The reason Amazon Advertising has been such a game changer for self-published authors is three-fold.

1. The visibility it gives our titles in the very place customers have come to browse and buy books — this is a whole different world from Facebook where users have so many other distractions.
2. It puts us on a level playing field with all publishers for online promotion in a way that was once impossible to achieve — previously Amazon only accepted traditional publisher advertisers with physical stock to sell. Happily those days have gone.
3. The cost to run Amazon ads is not prohibitive and is easy to control. You can start with budgets as low as $5 a day and pause your ads at any time.

Getting started with Amazon Advertising:

- go to your KDP dashboard
- choose 'Marketing' from the tabs at the top
- under 'Amazon Advertising' choose the country in which you'd like to start running your ads

If you write in English I'd recommend the US, UK and Canada to start with, taking on one at a time while you find your feet — I talk about the other territories later.

Returning to the ads dashboard after set-up:

- go to advertising.amazon.com
- choose 'sign in'
- from the dropdown enter the country whose ads dashboard you wish to access

Once you're set up in each territory you'll find that you can switch between European dashboards after signing in, using the dropdown top right on your desktop screen. Similarly you can switch between the US, Canada and Mexico when signed into one of those. These options may change.

Types of Amazon ads: at a glance

The Amazon ad types *relevant for children's authors* are:

1. **Sponsored Products Ads**
2. **Sponsored Brand Ads**

You'll also find **Lockscreen Ads** as an option in the ads dashboard. However, these appear **only** on Kindle readers, and so generally aren't suitable for our needs.

1. Sponsored Product Ads

These allow you to target your ads in three different ways:

- **Keyword targeting (manual)**
- **Product targeting (manual)** *(ASIN and category targeting)*
- **Automatic targeting**

Note: In the US only (at the time of writing) you can choose to add custom text to your Sponsored Product Ads. If you look at children's books on the US store then scroll down to the ads carousel you'll see examples of this. See later for more on custom text.

1.1 Keyword targeting

In forums you will often hear this ad type referred to as 'Sponsored Keyword Ad'.

With this manual targeting option, you select a book to advertise then choose 'keywords' — single words, or phrases — that you think customers may be using when searching for a book like yours. Search terms can be general or specific. For example, as a general search term you might enter 'children's Christmas book' with the aim of getting your book to show in results for that search term. Or 'Chapter book age 7' if you want to target customers looking for this type of book. And if you want to target a specific book that you feel is a good match for your own book you might (for example) enter *'The Christmasaurus' or 'Tom Fletcher the Christmasaurus'.*

While you can add up to 1,000 keywords for each campaign, a couple of hundred is probably enough to start with.

1.2 Product Targeting — ASINs and Categories

With this manual targeting option you have two choices:

- **Individual product ads** (often referred to in forums as '**ASIN ads'**) — you laser target your ad to appear on the product detail page for *specific* books you have chosen, identified by their unique Amazon Standard ID Number (ASIN) — note that there are separate ASINs for eBook and paperback formats

and / or

- **Category ads** — you target your ad to appear when customers are browsing Amazon children's book categories that you think are a good fit for your book

I talk about choosing and grouping targets, and how ASIN ads differ from keyword ads for book titles, in the later section *Manual ads - targeting tips.*

1.3 Automatic Targeting *('Auto Ads')*

Automatic ads require little input from you at the outset beyond daily budget, maximum keyword bid, and perhaps the addition of a couple of negative keywords (on which more in the later section *Optimising your Amazon ads*).

In order to decide where to run auto ads, Amazon looks at your book's dashboard metadata from set-up. This will include the seven keywords/keyword phrases you were asked to input, the reader age / school grade range you entered, which two main categories you chose and any others you added later, your book's title and any subtitle, and the keywords and phrases in your book description. It then shows your ad in the search results or on the detail pages of similar or loosely matching products. *(See the checklist in Chapter 18 for choosing up to 10 book categories.)*

Auto ads also look at any sales history, which will tell it which keywords and search terms have previously led to good click-through rates and sales — and it may (I am guessing) also look at keywords in customer reviews.

If you're advertising a new book, clearly there will be no sales or reviews history. In this case Amazon's algorithm will need time to learn which search terms and keywords deliver sales and which don't — and will rely fully on your base metadata to set if off in the right direction. If that metadata is way off, your auto ad risks stalling because it will struggle to get clicks. This is why **relevancy in your book's metadata is king**! Don't be tempted to game the system by including irrelevant but popular keywords during set-up in the hope of getting more visibility for your book as it's likely to backfire!

Although Amazon automatically targets these ads for you, once they are up and running you can make adjustments to improve their performance. I cover this in the later section *Optimising your Amazon ads*.

2. Sponsored Brand Ads

Note: I would leave experimenting with these until after you are confident with Sponsored Product Ads.

The main aim of Sponsored Brand Ads is to drive discovery of your overall offering and find new customers. You'll need at least three books in order to use this ad type.

When setting them up in the KDP dashboard, you can display your author image or imprint logo, a short custom headline, and three of your books. *(These options are at the time of writing but may change over time.)*

The ads appear in a variety of prominent places on Amazon, and if a customer clicks the ad they go to a simple landing page which lists three or more titles that you've selected. Below is a screenshot of a sample ad on Amazon in the US.

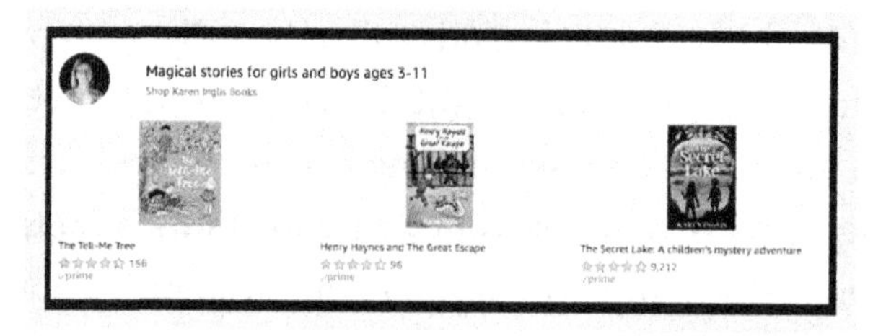

Sponsored brand ad shows three books

And here's how my landing page for this ad looks if a customer clicks through.

Example landing page for a brand ad

Organising and naming campaigns

Hierarchy

The ads dashboard hierarchy goes like this: **Campaign > Ad Group > Ad** and the performance stats are shown at these three levels.

Ad Groups allow you to run ads for different products (books or box sets) using the same set of keywords or product targets as the other ads in that same group. This can work well if you have books in a series or collection where the keywords are closely aligned. As all of my books are standalone, with differing keyword needs, there's no incentive for me to do this. Not using Ad Groups also means that when I log in I can see how each individual ad is performing at a glance at the top page (campaign level) without having to drill down to the Ad level. As a result, my Campaign name is the same as my Ad name. When I want to make keyword adjustments or read search reports for an ad *(covered later)*, I simply click on the Campaign, then on past the 'Ad Group' label to get to the individual ad's dashboard page. Here I can access the relevant more detailed stats.

Naming convention

Here's how I *aim* to name my various ads.

Auto ad with custom text (US store only)

Book initials_Auto_format_ Custom Text Version_text hint

- TSL_AutoP_CT01_summer read
- TSL_AutoP&E_CT02_mystery adventure

Auto Ads (no custom text)

Book initials_Auto_format

- TSL_Auto_pb
- TSL Auto_eBook
- TSL_Auto_P&E

Sponsored Keyword Ad (Manual)

Book initials_ad type_format_keyword type

- TSL_SPA_P_genres
- TSL_SPA_E_comp titles/authors

Product Ads — ASINs

Book initials_format_ ad type_targeting hint

- TSL_P_ASIN_ adventure
- TSL_P_ASIN_ historical fiction

Product Ads — Categories

Book initials_Format_CAT

- TSL_P&E_CAT

If you choose to run the ads to separate categories you can, of course, add a category hint into the name. This all becomes clear at set-up.

• • •

Sponsored Brand Ads

Brand_3 titles_ text hint_target hint

- Brand_TSL/WB/EK_ magical tales_comp ASINs

Budget and bidding — at a glance

When setting up your ad you'll be asked to:

- set a daily budget for your campaign
- decide on your bidding strategy (dynamic bids — down only; dynamic bids — up and down, or fixed bids)
- choose how much you want to bid for each keyword, product or category for manual ads

How much and 'how' should you bid?

When starting out your safest bet is to:

- choose 'dynamic bids down'
- set a daily budget of no more than you can afford to lose — I'd recommend $10 to get you going
- choose bids of no more than 0.35/0.35p — I explain below why this doesn't necessarily mean a click will *cost* you this much

Tip 1: Within each ad type it's simplest to ***set a default bid*** at the outset and have it apply for all your targets. You can adjust it later where necessary, once you've seen how those targets are performing.

Tip 2: ***ignore Amazon recommendations for bids*** — these are often ridiculously high. If authors all followed these suggestions, we'd price ourselves out of the market!

How the bidding auction works

- For each keyword / product (book) / category you choose you set the maximum cost per click that you're willing to pay for your ad to show.

- Once your ad is running, and as customers are searching online for books, each of your bids enters a live 'auction' with other advertisers using the same targets — your aim is to get your ad to show before or instead of those of your competitors.

- The book with the 'winning bid' is placed either top of search (for general keywords), or first place in the 'Sponsored products' row on the product page of the book you were targeting. This row in turn usually sits below a row entitled 'Customers also bought' or 'Books you may like' or similar. (Amazon is constantly playing with names when trying to cross market so these labels names may change.) In forums you'll often see the ads row referred to as the **'ads carousel'** because you can scroll through it horizontally and eventually come full circle.

- Winning bids are selected based on a combination of **bid price, how relevant Amazon thinks your book**

is for that search term and **your book's sales history from that search term**. Thus bidding high won't always win you first place — and if your book is new to Amazon it may take time for it to earn a place high up in the results, even if your bid is extremely high, because the algorithm has no history to go on.

- The minimum you can bid is 0.02 cents or 0.02 pence, but in order to gain impressions when starting out it's best practice to start higher — around 0.25c/p-0.35c/p, but that doesn't necessarily mean you'll pay that much because…

- …if someone clicks on your ad it will only ever cost you one cent or one pence more than the next highest bid for that keyword. Thus if you bid 0.30 cents on a given keyword and the next highest bid below this is for 0.20 cents, and Amazon ranks you above them because it thinks your ad is relevant, you'll only be charged 0.21cents if someone clicks on your ad.

- As you would expect, the ad that comes second in the auction will appear second place in ads carousel or as the second promoted product in search results — and so on.

Bidding and relevancy

It's worth emphasising again that, no matter what you bid for your keywords or related titles, if your book doesn't sell or get clicks, Amazon will in time stop showing your promotion — they firmly put their customers' needs first.

Ads targeting – getting started

Note: *For keyword ads, you can choose different 'match types' for your keywords – 'broad' 'exact' or 'phrase'. I explain these choices at the end of this section, though I do reference them below. Feel free to skip to that last sub-section then pop back if you'd rather read the definitions first.*

Starter ad campaigns

What follows is how I start out when I have a new title. Others, I am sure, will do it differently.

- For each book I initially create **two sponsored keyword ads** and **one automatic ad**. If the ad is in the US, I use Custom Text.

- **I create one campaign for each ad** — I don't make use of Ad Groups within a campaign as I prefer to see all info for each ad I'm running at the top level on the ads dashboard. This means that during set-up I just click through the 'Ad Group' label and ignore it. *(Nb all my book are standalones – if you write in a series there may be a good case for grouping them under one campaign, and I suggest you read around on this!)*

- For my manual keyword ads, I choose **'broad' keywords** and **set the default bid at 0.35c/35p**, or less sometimes. (See the next section for more on keyword types.)

- **For my auto ads** I add as **negative keywords** my author name and the book's title (and close variations on these which Amazon helpfully suggests), and as **negative products** the book's print and eBook ASINs. I do this as I want to use my auto ads to discover which books and search terms *customers who don't know me* are using when looking for books like mine. This approach not only saves me unnecessary paid-for clicks, it allows me to harvest more search terms from potential new customers to use in my manual ads.

- After a couple of weeks with a new ad I then go in and look at the sales and search term reports to see what is and isn't working and refine from there. See more on this in *Optimising your Amazon ads.*

- Thereafter, depending on how the ads above are performing, I may go in and create separate Product ads (one ASIN ad and one Category ad) for the book. However, I don't like to confuse myself or have too many things to monitor so will only try these options if I can't get the other ads to make money or at the very least break even.

With the at-a-glance overview out of the way, let's now look at how I choose and group my keywords when creating manual ads.

. . .

Manual ads — combining Amazon suggestions with your research

Reminder: manual ads include Sponsored Keyword Ads, Product Ads (ASINs and Categories), and Sponsored Display Ads.

Depending on the ad type — and to help you get started — Amazon puts forward suggestions of keywords, competitor books and/or book categories for you to target. These suggestions are based on what it knows about your book from the metadata you included at set-up, as described earlier, and/or from any sales history.

You can ignore or cherry pick from these Amazon suggestions, then use the available tabs to add or search for more, and/or to paste in or upload your own pre-researched list of keywords, or ASINs. I talk below about my keyword research.

Usefully, if you manually type in keywords to add Amazon will suggest yet more — as happens when a customer searches on Amazon — and you can, of course pick and choose from these. ***Tip:*** *Keep your ads relevant by avoiding suggestions that clearly are not a good fit for your book!*

Researching and grouping keywords (keyword ads)

My first keyword ad will focus on **general keywords that relate to my book's genre and target reading age** — so, for *Eeek! The Runaway Alien* I might include phrases such as:

- Chapter book
- Book age 7

- Book age 8
- Funny book for boys
- Early reader
- Second grade book
- Soccer story ages 7-10
- Alien children's book

For *The Secret Lake* I might include:

- Adventure story age 8
- Time travel for kids
- Historical fiction children's book
- Middle grade adventure

My second keyword ad will focus on **books similar to mine or the names of authors whose books are similar in theme or feel to mine**. You can find these by browsing online to see what's selling in categories where your book appears. Once your book is selling, you can also harvest ideas from the list of 'Customers also read' that usually shows on your book's product page.

Thus for Eeek! I might include:

- Diary of a Wimpy Kid
- Books by Jeff Kinney
- Cheeky Charlie books
- Captain Underpants
- Dave Pilkey books
- The Boy Who Dreamed of Dragons

For *The Secret Lake* I might include:

- Enid Blyton
- Nancy Drew books
- Five Get Into Trouble
- Tom's Midnight Garden
- The Secret Garden
- The Virginia Mysteries
- Steven Smith books

There are free and paid-for tools that will help you research and 'scrape' book titles and author keywords from Amazon category pages and other sites such as Goodreads. Other tools will create keyword lists from suggestions you input, or by drawing on search terms used on Amazon or Google. See the later section *'Tools to help with your keyword research'*.

The above said, without a doubt my most successful keyword ads have been those based on my manual research — browsing relevant categories on Amazon then cherry picking the books that feel a good fit for the title I am advertising. I also look at new releases when doing this. Web scraping tools can make this task faster up to a point, but you still need to separate the wheat from the chaff if there's a mix of relevant and less relevant titles on the page!

The Amazon suggestions that come up in the search bar on the main site and in the suggestions field within the ads console when you start typing a keyword are extremely useful for keyword list creation. However, I've had less success with the keyword generation tools as there's been too much to sift through that doesn't relate to children's books.

Auto ads – set up and negative targeting

Aside from entering your campaign budget and default keyword bid, there's not much to do with auto ads, as Amazon will do the targeting for you. However, as mentioned earlier, I'd recommend including your author name and the book's title and ASIN as negative keywords and negative products at this time. This stops the auto ad from being shown to customers who know you already and will help it focus on finding new customers whose other search terms you can harvest for your manual ads.

THE FIVE KEYWORD MATCH TYPES

With **keyword ads** you get to choose between a range of **keyword match types**. These allow you to fine-tune which customer search terms will or won't fire up your ads.

The definitions below are closely drawn from the KDP help text:

- **Broad match:** contains all the keywords in any order and includes plurals, variations and related keywords.
- **Phrase match:** Contains the exact phrase or sequence of keywords. Also includes the plural form of the keyword. Because it's more restrictive than broad match, phrase match will generally result in more relevant placements for your ad.

- **Exact match:** Must exactly match the keyword or sequence of keywords in order for the ad to show, but will also match close variations of the exact term. The most restrictive match type, but can be more relevant for a search. Includes the plural form of the keyword. *(I agree there are a few contradictions in here!)*

You can also add **negative keywords**, which will prevent your ad from being shown if a customer types in a particular search term or close variation. Again, the definitions that follow are from KDP's help text.

- **Negative phrase:** Ads don't show on shopping queries that contain the complete phrase or close variations.
- **Negative exact:** Ads don't show on shopping queries that contain the exact phrase or close variation.

You can add any keyword type at set-up or later on — and you can pause them at any time.

Optimising your Amazon ads: getting started

Optimising is all about making tweaks to increase your return on investment (profits) from your ads. Below I share what I do once my ads have been running for a few weeks and how I keep an eye on longer term ads. Note that what works for one book or one author doesn't work for others — but we can all learn from each other. Also, Amazon is constantly making changes to the advertising features and targeting options it offers. To keep on top of what's changing I recommend you join the Facebook Group '*Authors Optimizing Amazon and Facebook Ads - Support Group*'. I also highly recommend Deb Potter's book *Amazon Ads for Authors* and Robert J Ryan's book *Amazon Ads Unleashed*. I've added these to the recommended resources area at the end of this chapter. In the meantime, the fundamentals below should, at the very least, set you in the right direction.

Monitoring impressions, clicks and orders

After three or four days I check to see if I'm getting impressions — if I'm not I may increase the daily budget to try to get things moving. This may involve increasing it to $50/£50 a day or higher. Some authors suggest adding a campaign end date to get things moving. I don't do this — you may wish to try. If things still aren't moving, check your metadata from set-up. Is it relevant for your title?

Continuing over the first week or two I keep a daily eye just to be sure nothing's going haywire — such as Amazon burning all my money with high cost clicks on a keyword with no evidence of orders after three or four days. If that starts to happen, I'll reduce the keyword bid and keep a closer eye on it. *It takes three days for orders to show up so don't adjust too soon where you're getting clicks but no orders.*

Note: most authors struggle to get Amazon to spend their daily budget and many clicks come in at below your bid price for the reasons mentioned earlier. But I feel that if I don't keep a daily eye on new campaigns in the first week or two, I'll get caught out. It's also a good way to check you didn't accidentally bid $35 or £35 for a keyword instead of $0.35 / £0.35 — I've been there and done that and had the £45 bill to pay the next morning! On that note, see the later section *Tips to avoid accidentally overbidding.*

Pausing or reducing bids on underperforming keywords

During the first month I'll keep checking — and pausing keywords that are clearly not performing. My rule of thumb here is that 15-20 clicks and no order means the keyword isn't working. Some authors pause after 10 clicks and no order. I tend to leave it longer *if the click cost isn't high,* especially if the keyword is giving me lots of impressions — the visibility my book is getting offers a cheap form of advertising creating brand awareness. And at some stage north of 10 clicks at a low price I will invariably suddenly get an order that gives me a profitable sale.

Amazon likes to give customers what they want. For that reason, the perceived wisdom is that if you leave an ad that has lots of keywords with no clicks for too long, Amazon may decide the overall ad campaign isn't relevant, and start showing it less frequently and eventually stop it running. If you see impressions start to fall off at the campaign level, best practice is to pause those keywords and let the ad focus on the good keywords.

In the same breath, I should add that if a campaign is performing well overall (meaning I'm making money on it) I will often leave keywords running that have had lots of impressions and no clicks, as I see this as form of free advertising.

In short, there are contradictions in the system that I can't explain — so it's a case of using your gut instinct some of the time!

Using 'breakeven ACOS' to work out if I'm making money

While monitoring clicks and order rates, I simultaneously look at the ACOS (Average Cost of Sales figure — Total Ad Spend/Total Sales expressed as a percentage) in the ads dashboard.

However, note that **ACOS is misleading for authors as it stands, as it's based on the sale price rather than the royalty you will receive from the sale.** To adjust for this, I have a chart where I work out my 'breakeven' ACOS for a sale of each of my print books **based on its royalty** then use those breakeven figures as a benchmark. If the ACOS rises above the breakeven figure for that book, I know the ad / keyword is losing me money. If things stay that way for long, I'll go in and either drastically reduce bids on costly keywords or pause them altogether. If things are way off, I'll pause the ad altogether.

I recommend you set up your own ACOS chart for your print books. See below for how to do this. (It's much simpler for eBooks — in this case the ACOS breakeven figure is typically 70%, meaning anything below this puts you in profit. If you get lots of page reads, breakeven can be higher. Our focus, however, is on print books.)

Tip: When looking at ACOS, be aware that it can take a few days for orders to start showing up in the ads dash — so don't jump to conclusions about how your ad is performing if it shows a high ACOS at the start. Once an ad is up and running, I tend to use the 14-day sales period as my rule of thumb benchmark for how things are doing. If you're just looking over the past few days the ACOS will look high because the orders may not have been posted yet.

Calculating your breakeven ACOS percentage for print sales

- Check your print book royalty in the KDP bookshelf
- Divide the royalty by the on-sale price (RRP or discount price if Amazon has reduced it)
- Multiply the result by 100
- This is your ACOS breakeven percentage.

Example

I keep a spreadsheet for each book and add a column with the new temporary ACOS if Amazon discounts it.

Royalty/On-sale Price =Paperback

	THE SECRET LAKE				
	RRP	PB Royalty	PB Breakeven	Offer Price	Offer price break-even
USA	7.99	2.48	31.04%		
UK	6.99	2.27	32.47%	6.15	36.91%
DE	6.99	2.13	30.47%		
FR	6.99	2.13	30.47%		
SPAIN	6.99	2.13	30.47%		
ITALY	6.99	2.13	30.47%		
Japan	895	118	13.18%		
CA	10.55	3.27	31.00%		

ACOS breakeven % increases if Amazon discounts the book – anything at or below this means the ad isn't losing money

Ads dash orders vs KDP Sales Reports numbers

Note that book orders show up in the ads dashboard before the book is shipped, so aren't usually included in what the separate KDP Sales Report page is telling you today. That report only includes shipped books. There can be a lag of up to three to seven days, sometimes longer, between order and shipping. It partly depends on whether the buyer is in Amazon Prime and partly on whether it's a holiday season, or if other factors are at play such as delays due to Covid.

Also, remember that the KDP Sales Reports will include all sales — not just those that result from your ads. Thus — depending on how extensively you are advertising elsewhere, and/or how well your Amazon ads are performing — the firm sales figures here may be substantially higher than the order numbers showing in the ads dash.

For example, I haven't typically advertised a lot outside of Amazon, yet I've seen my KDP sales (as seen in the reports) for a given month run at between 30% and 75% higher than the ads dash order numbers. In most cases I can't put those extra sales down to external ads, so my assumption is these extras are organic sales as a result of word of mouth recommendations that in turn trace back to previous sales triggered by ads. For this reason, even if an ad is only just breaking even, as long as the KDP report's sales match or exceed the orders showing in the ad dash (once the ad has been running for two or three weeks) I keep the ad running in the hope that organic sales will creep up over the longer term. In most cases — thanks to optimising — my ads are already more than breaking even.

Using search term reports to optimise ad campaigns

One of the best ways to analyse ad performance, beyond viewing what's happening on the ads dash, is to view current and historical search term reports. At the time of writing you can get to these in two ways once inside the campaign manager:

- Click through to the ad you want to analyse (ie past the 'Ad Group' level to the ad itself if you're not using groups), then choose 'search terms' from the left hand pane.

or

- Click on the three horizontal white bars on the black background top left of the campaigns manager screen, then choose reports. Here you can request a range of reports — not just search term. Detailing them all is outside the scope of this book and would become far too complicated. (I've not delved into all of them myself!) Read the Amazon help text and explore the resources I recommend in this chapter to understand more. Best practice is to make a point of running and downloading the ones you find most useful at the start of each month, as you can only ever go back 65 days.

In what follows, and to keep things simple, I'll focus on the search reports you can see from the left hand menu at the ad level, ie the first option above.

1. Search term reports for manual ads

Reminder: manual ads include Sponsored Keyword Ads, Product Ads (ASINs and Categories), and Sponsored Display Ads.

When you click on the 'search terms' option in the left-hand menu at the ad level, depending on the ad type you'll see either a list of customer search terms (if it's a sponsored keyword ad) or a list of books on whose detail pages your auto ad appeared (if it's an ASIN or Category ad).

1.1 Harvesting productive search terms

Use the available sorting columns to find any customer search terms that resulted in decent orders and a good ACOS over a given period, then add those search terms or books as new keywords or product targets into your campaign. There's an 'Actions' prompt that allows you to do this directly from this search report page, and you can select multiple terms to add in one go if you wish.

Tip: Be sure to select 'default bid' when adding these terms — not the 'suggested' bid that Amazon will put forward when you go to complete the task. For keyword and ASIN ads in particular their suggestion is likely to be considerably higher than your existing default bid for that ad.

For sponsored keyword ads, you'll also need to decide if you want to make your new terms 'broad', 'exact' or 'phrase' keywords. I'd say what's best will depend on how many impressions that customer search term has had. If it's a high number it may be worth going for 'exact' to try to capitalise on that term, otherwise choose 'broad' or 'phrase'. As with everything, test it and see — and read the recommended resources where you'll find more nuanced advice than I can offer! Remember: you can always adjust later.

1.2 Negating poorly performing keywords

Conversely, for keywords that you can see are costing you money but not generating sales, add them as negative keywords to prevent your ad showing up when a customer enters that term. Again, Amazon prompts you to show you how to do this.

Example: customer search terms such as 'free children's books', 'kindle books for kids' or 'board books for toddlers' might be triggering your ad to show because you have the broad match keywords 'children's books' 'books for kids' or 'books for toddlers' in your ad. But if you're not advertising free books, kindle books or board books you clearly don't want clicks wasted on those terms! Other culprits might be a particular author's set of books which you can see from the search reports are being matched with your ad and getting lots of clicks but no sales — even though the target age range is the same.

1.3 Should you negate your name and book in manual ads?

Search reports often show that customers have clicked on your ad after entering your name or book in search. In this case clearly that sale has cost you money when they'd have found your book anyway.

There are two schools of thought on this. Some welcome it, and indeed add their names and books as keywords from the outset to try to prevent competitors' ads displaying next to their book and diverting buyers away. Using 'selfie' keywords in this way is called 'defensive advertising'.

Other authors are having none of this! Instead they add their names and books as negative keywords or products, to make sure their ad never shows when a customer searches for them.

This is for you to weigh up and decide on. Defensive advertising has been around for many moons and there is good reason for it. In case it helps, I have found the CPC on 'selfie' keywords to be quite low, thus resulting in a low ACOS, presumably because Amazon views the term as highly relevant for my product!

Where it can mislead in the early days, however, is by making your overall campaign ACOS look low when most of that is down to customers already searching for your books. As your campaigns gain a longer shelf life — and as you continue to optimise — this hidden imbalance becomes less significant. One thought (as I write!) to avoid being seduced by a low ACOS when starting a new campaign, is that you could *start* by negating your name and book, then cancelling that option and adding your title / author name as a keyword once the ad settles down. This would definitely make sense if you see major competitors targeting your book with Sponsored Brand Ads.

2. Search term reports for auto ads

When you look at search reports for auto ads, you'll see a list of books on whose detail pages your auto ad appeared. In addition, at the end or sprinkled in between, you may find a list of customer search terms that triggered your auto ad.

Again, use the available sorting columns to see which terms resulted in decent orders and ACOS over a given period, then — if they're not there already — add those books or search terms to one of your manual sponsored product ads. The advantage of having these known performing terms in your manual ads is that you can increase the bids on them with the aim of scaling sales. With auto ads you can't set individual bids for individual keywords or products.

2.1 De-duplicating harvested auto ad keywords

Best practice says that at this stage you should now add the above 'harvested' terms as negative keywords or negative products for your auto ad going forward — so they don't compete with the duplicate keywords in your manual ads. While I'm sure this is sensible advice, it's not something I do *if my auto ad is making me money* — I live in fear of upsetting the applecart on ads that are performing well! (Yes, I'm a coward when it comes to upsetting the algorithm — I'm afraid you'll need to decide on this for yourself!)

2.2 Negating costly auto ad keywords or products

If you see from an auto ad search term report that a particular book or search term is getting lots of impressions and clicks (and so costing you money) but not leading to any or many sales you can improve performance by entering this as a negative search term or product in your auto ad campaign. Your auto ad will no longer show up for those terms and your return on investment should improve.

2.3 Negating keywords that relate to you / your product in auto ads

Tip: It's a good idea at the outset with auto ads to add your book's title and your author name as negative keywords and phrases, because you really want to use auto ads to *find new customers and new targeting options*. Your focus should be on harvesting any profitable keywords for use in other ads.

2.4 Monitoring Amazon's match types for auto ads

With automatic targeting, Amazon displays our ads to shoppers who are searching not just for products it believes are a close match for our book, but also ones that are a loose match, or complementary to it, or a possible substitute for it. These definitions in the context of books are hard to wrap our heads around (and I think are really designed for other product types) — but it's important you're aware of them, Why? Because once your auto ad is running you can view, adjust or pause any of these four targeting tactics depending on how they're performing.

To view these options, select 'Targeting' from the left-hand pane when you're at the auto ad level.

As you will see in the following screenshot, you get all the usual performance information in the associated columns, including CTR, orders and ACOS. Once or twice I've found that 'loose match' has been costing me fruitless clicks over an extended period and so have paused it. In another ad, I was making sales but at a fairly high ACOS, so I drastically lowered the bid for that match type. This improved the overall performance for that auto ad. Where match types are not showing any impressions over an extended period I turn them off for good measure.

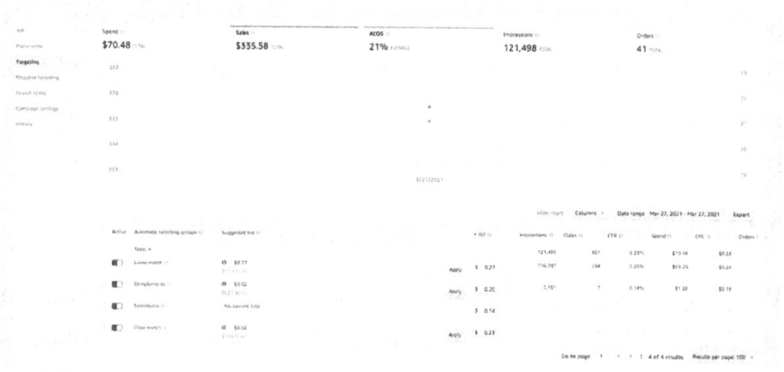

Auto ad match types - adjust or pause bids depending on performance — also in the resources folder

Custom text in US Ads — should you use it?

I always include custom text with my US sponsored product ads as it offers me a chance to hint at reading age for the title. This can reduce wasted clicks and/or may catch the attention of someone searching for a book in the specific ages range.

Thus for *The Secret Lake* I may say 'A page-turning summer adventure for ages 8-11' or for my fox books 'A gentle rhyming story for ages 3-5'. This said, word from key

Amazon ads team experts is that Amazon itself hasn't found any better performance using custom text than not — and my ads certainly don't perform any worse in the UK or other territories where it's not an option. This is one for you to decide on! You could try testing the same book with and without custom text of course, though I wonder if this might dilute the effectiveness of both ads as they would be competing for the same keywords.

Tools to help you find keywords

Amazon Suggestions

Make the most of the suggestions that come up when you start to type a search term into Amazon. Similarly, look at the autogenerated search terms that appear when you start to type a keyword into the targeting area for any manual Amazon ad. For best ad performance, remember to avoid keywords that aren't relevant for your book.

Publisher Rocket can help with Amazon Ads keyword research, albeit when using this for children's books I've often found myself having to unpick a lot of books for YA or adults that came back in the results. Even so, Publisher Rocket is worth considering because it's so good for category and competitor research. The cost is $97 + VAT (2021). Find out more at **bit.ly/RocketKarenInglis**, or search online.

Pickasin

This free tool helps you quickly collect Amazon ASINs from search results lists — useful if you want to cherry pick specific books then copy and paste the ASINs into a Product

(ASIN) ad. Unfortunately it doesn't work on category pages - only search results pages. Find out more **pickasin.com**

BKLNK

At the time of writing, this free tool allows you to collect the top 50 ASINS for any given category. I'd still sift these to remove those not relevant for your book. Visit **BKLNK.com**

Webscraper Chrome extension

This Chrome extension allows you to visit any web page (including Amazon category pages) and scrape a list of book titles that you can then copy and paste into Excel. You'll need to 'clean up' the keyword data in Excel by removing any punctuation marks etc that Amazon doesn't like — and taking out any titles you don't think are relevant. Once this is done you can paste the list into a keyword ad. This is a great way to hand-pick book titles for Sponsored Keyword Ads from Amazon category pages. A fellow author from the Self-publishing Formula group kindly put together a simple video showing how to use this. You'll find it at **bit.ly/easywebscrape**

Tips to avoid accidentally overbidding

ALERT! It's very easy to make mistakes when changing or choosing bids, especially late at night when you're tired, or if you're distracted or in a hurry! Follow these rules to avoid costly errors:

- If you've made *any* change to your bids, or if you've just set up a new ad, before signing off, click in the header of the 'Bid' column once, then once again.

This will sort your bids for the whole campaign first by ascending and then by descending order. That way, if you've accidentally added a bid for $15, for example, it will be clearly visible at the top of the descending sort results.

- Any bulk action to make changes to keyword or ASIN bids only applies to the page you're looking at — it doesn't ripple through. Thus, if you want to change *all bids* down or up to a new amount using the bulk checkbox, be sure to click through and separately apply this on *all pages*. If you don't, the change will only apply to the keywords on the page you are viewing. **Tip:** Ask Amazon to show you 300 results per page (the maximum it will display at the time of writing), then apply the change to that page. Then go to the next page and repeat and so on if you have more than 300 keywords.

- When setting up your ads, be sure to change **Amazon's 'Suggested bid'** (seen in the first screenshot that follows) to **your preferred 'Default bid'**. If you don't, it will price all keywords you add now and at later dates at its normally inflated 'suggested bid'. You need to click the drop-down and choose 'Default' — the last option — then adjust what is there to your preferred bid amount. (Note that it will pre-populate with a high default bid. You will typically be reducing that to 0.35c/p or less, to start with at least.)

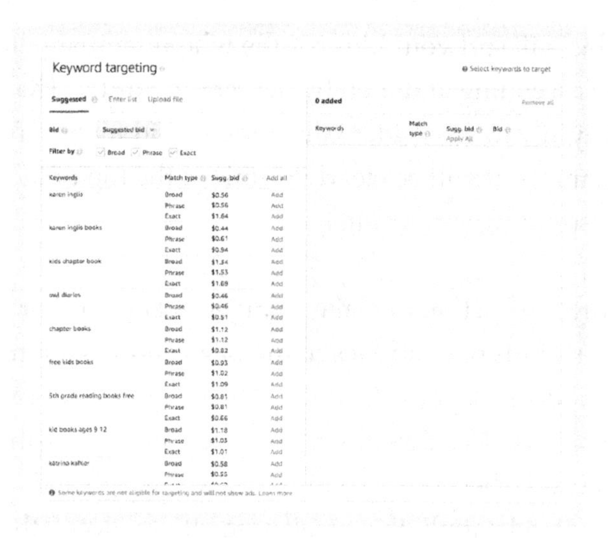

Decide on your Default Bid and enter it at the outset

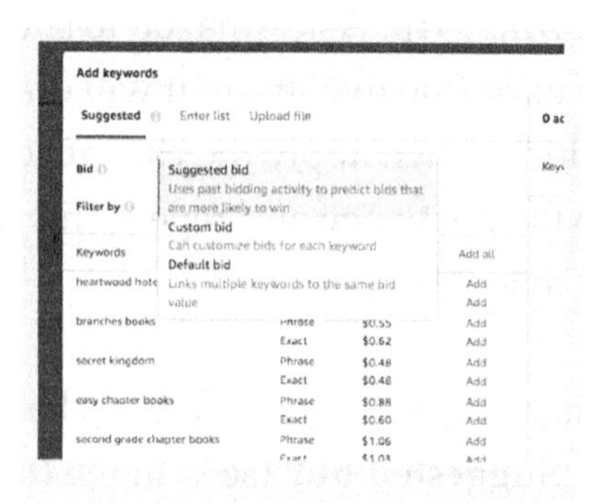

Select and adjust 'Default Bid' from the dropdown

However, don't relax yet. Amazon not only pre-populates the default bid with a high amount (0.75c in this case) if you forgot to set it earlier, it also pre-ticks all three match types for the keyword(s) you are adding. I would start out just using 'broad', which you hope will harvest you related keywords in the search term report.

All match types are ticked by default - deselect those you don't need, and change your default bid to 0.35 or below.

- Look out for this again when you come back at a later date to add new keywords. **At every opportunity Amazon will auto display its suggested bid and pre-tick all three match types.** It is very easy to miss this when tired or in a hurry. I've been there and done that on all counts!

Amazon ads — further resources

Over time, as you learn what's working or not working for your ads, you will want to adjust and refine your wider strategy, and ideally find new ways to scale your ads — perhaps delving into some of the other report types. That level of detail is outside the scope of this book, but I hope I've at least set you in the right direction. To complement my high level guidance, here are some recommended resources.

HIGHLY RECOMMENDED READING

- *Amazon Ads for Authors* by Deb Potter
- *Amazon Ads Unleashed* by Robert J Ryan

FACEBOOK GROUPS

- *'Authors Optimizing Amazon and Facebook Ads - Support Group'*
- *'Author unleashed' — in depth discussion on ad tactics, run by Robert J Ryan (see above)*

AMAZON ADS ONLINE TRAINING

- *Advertising for Authors course, Self-publishing Formula:* If you have budget to spare and wish to leave no stone unturned, take a look at the above course. Aimed at intermediate to advanced level it covers *a lot more* than Amazon Advertising, including Facebook and BookBub ads. Its comprehensive Amazon Advertising module is designed and run by a senior ex Amazon Ads team member, Janet Margot. Caveat: as I write, the ads course *is not aimed at children's or print books,* but its overall strategies are relevant for all authors. And if you happen to be a middle grade author selling a lot of eBooks in a series, you'll find extensive detail about calculating read-through. A good, high quality course that is regularly updated, but I'd say one to consider once you're well into your marketing journey and already making a steady income. Find out more at **selfpublishingformula.com/marketing**

- *Sell More Books with Amazon Ads, Dave Chesson — free:* From the brains behind the *Publisher Rocket* software this free five-part self-serve course will help get you up and running with Amazon ads and introduce you to how the Publisher Rocket tool can help you locate categories and keywords. Find out more at: **bit.ly/DC_Ads** (*Disclosure: this is an affiliate link should you later choose to buy Publisher Rocket.)*

- *Bryan Cohen's Five-Day Amazon Ads Challenge — free:* Another free course (runs live on given dates) that will help you get started if you're new to Amazon ads — good for understanding the basics in walk-through videos. Includes crafting copy hooks for ads that allow custom text, and the ability to get feedback from fellow authors in the related Facebook group. Caution: When I took this course Bryan recommended that you create multiple ads for the same book to get things moving. I personally don't advise this as your ads dash will become overwhelming. I'd stick to far fewer ads and optimise those. But that's just my opinion! Expect cross-sell to paid versions of the course but there's no obligation. Search online: **Bryan Cohen Five-Day Amazon Ads Challenge.**

Podcasts

- Listen to **Self-publishing Podcast Episode 128** where Canadian children's author Laurie Wright talks about the success she's had with Amazon ads. An old interview but you'll still find some nuggets in there. (The follow-on **podcast 129** is with me and covers all aspects of children's publishing and marketing, ahead of the launch of this book.)

Final takeaways on Amazon Advertising

Research your keywords carefully and advertise against books and authors that are genuinely a good 'fit' with yours — this is where I seem to get the best results.

Use automatic targeting to harvest new keywords for your manual ads — but make sure your book's metadata is correct and relevant, to give the auto ad the best chance of matching your book with relevant shoppers.

Don't bid more than you can afford to lose.

Facebook advertising

I first experimented with simple Facebook ads way back in 2013, spending $5 a day over a week or so, aiming mainly for page likes for *The Secret Lake,* as everything I had read told me that Facebook users didn't like being taken off the platform. The page got lots of likes, but I really wasn't sure what to do with them and was still busy in my day job in any event! I also ran a few ads to the book's Amazon page. With no obvious impact on sales, I shelved the idea.

I tried again on and off between 2016-2020, during which time the range of ads types had become more sophisticated, offering not just single images but also carousel ads, video ads, lead generation ads, awareness ads, website traffic and conversion ads and so on. Audience targeting had also become more sophisticated, giving you the option to narrow down not just by location and demographic but also by interest and buying behaviour.

In a nutshell — and with one exception that I'll go on to cover shortly — while this form of advertising has worked extremely well for many authors of adult and YA books, it has continued to be a challenge for me. Most children's authors I know (of books for up to age 12) who have tried Facebook ads have the same story and I think this comes back to the fact that the buyers we are targeting (parents mostly) are not the book readers and so impulse buys are much harder to come by. They are also not on Facebook to buy books. Targeting grandparents is probably a better bet — especially around the holiday season and now I've dipped my toe back in (on which more in a moment!) this grandparent targeting is something I intend to try for Christmas 2021 with *The Christmas Tree Wish*. (I have previously tried targeting parents of children aged 6-12 with my middle grade books at Christmas and other times, but to no avail. Going with a Christmas themed book might work though…) Before I go on to talk about my recent one 'success' story with Facebook ads here are a couple of other exceptions.

Successful children's book Facebook ads — case studies

One of the few instances where I've heard of runaway success for fiction children's book Facebook ads is for the 'Lost My Name' and other personalised picture books published by Wonderbly. These have apparently sold millions off the back of Facebook ads. However, their marketing budget is huge (really huge) and they have a *very* niche product. Other personalised niche books may work on this basis — but these are hard to scale using print on demand!

Another long-term success I'm aware of is with a small indie children's publisher in the US who achieved hundreds of likes and engagement with their ads over the years, which I assume had knock-on for sales. Diversity has always been at the heart of that publisher's books — long before the spotlight fell more recently on its underrepresentation in mainstream children's books. I am guessing the publisher was smartly targeting families, teachers, librarians and other professionals with an active interest in diversity, or who belonged to parent groups with a relevant demographic profile, or who live in locations with a highly diverse demographic and so on.

The author/publisher also offered a chapter book series where the first book was often free on Kindle. I expect most parents went on to buy the print book and that in turn would have led to sales from the rest of the series. Good on them all round! Niche targeting is where I believe Facebook ads can work for children's authors, on which note here's what's happened in 2021.

The Tell-Me Tree — case study

In 2021 I have finally had success with **one** Facebook ad — for ***The Tell-Me Tree***. I think this is probably due to its specialist theme, and the *professional* targeting opportunities it gives me. ***The Tell-Me Tree*** is a rhyming story that invites children to share how they are feeling — whether happy, sad, or anywhere in between — with friends, family or trusted grown-ups. It includes activity pages where children can talk, write about and/or draw a picture of how they are feeling — as well as links to free download activities for use at home or in the classroom, and links for parents who may be worried about a child. Oh — and the illustrations are adorable!

I decided I would try Facebook ads because, whilst my manual and auto Amazon ads for the book (targeting similar themed books and relevant categories),had worked up to a point in the UK, sales had plateaued and started to fall after a couple of months. I wanted to try to halt the slide before things dropped off too drastically, as this would teach Amazon's algorithm to start ignoring my book! Efforts to optimise and refocus the existing ads weren't working, so my aim was to make the most of Facebook's ability to laser target specific audiences. In this case I was after **teachers** and **those who work in or have an interest in children's mental health**.

I was lucky to get a fantastic quote from one teacher that I was able to use in the FB creative, which I designed using Canva (a screenshot follows). I also broke a few old school rules. I included an image of the book in the ad (with me). I included text on the image, and I included extremely long ad text. These are all things often quoted as being ill advised! However, I went with my gut instinct as to what I thought would grab the interest of my target audience.

Having recently read of one other author having success with 'long copy' in his adult fiction ad, I felt further encouraged to do what felt right.

Advertising a book with a niche audience seems to work

So far the ad has worked very well in the UK where, at the time of writing, it has 286 likes, 119 comments and 156 shares.

As soon as it started running I saw UK sales of ***The Tell-Me Tree*** go back up again — nothing ground breaking, but certainly more than enough to cover the ad's costs. My longer term aim is to encourage organic growth and sales through word of mouth.

In the meantime I'll keep the ad running for as long as I'm not losing money.

For the record: I ran the same ad in the US and got good engagement, but zero sales! 'Go figure!' as they say. Needless to say, I stopped that ad.

Getting started with Facebook ads

A detailed look at how to set up and run Facebook Ads is outside the scope of this book. However, there is lots of free advice online.

I'd start with Reedsy's free course at **bit.ly/ReedsyFB** and/or take a looks at Dave Chesson's step-by step guide at **bit.ly/DaveChessonFB**

If, in time, Facebook ads work for you, there are more in-depth paid courses if you have budget, including Mark Dawson's excellent *Advertising for Authors* course.

However, be aware that (at the time of writing) most of these courses don't focus on children's books.

To stalk general conversations on optimising, join the Facebook group *'Authors Optimizing Amazon and Facebook Ads - Support Group'* — and search 'Facebook ads' in children's self-publishing groups.

Here are a few starter tips in the meantime.

Buyer beware when running Facebook ads

If you plan to test the waters with Facebook advertising, be aware that Facebook has a wonderful knack of eating your money! Costs per click have fluctuated wildly over recent years, so this is a space that I treat with caution. Crucially — and unlike with Amazon where you will often struggle to spend your daily budget — Facebook will gobble your money up! **What you budget is what you spend** so you really need to be sure your ad is relevant and making positive returns. Three to five days should be enough to assess how it's doing, so if you're going to try, keep to $5 a day to start with!

Use boosted posts to gain new followers for ad targeting and lookalike audience building

As I mentioned in Chapter 6 on social media marketing, occasional low-budget Facebook boosted 'engagement' posts from your author page are a good way to start building your brand in the early days. You can use these not only to increase engagement from existing followers (many of whom won't otherwise see your post), but also to target new audiences that you can specify at the boost set-up stage, based on age, gender, interests and so on — as you would for an ad. If someone new likes your post, you can then invite them to like your page — increasing your follow count and social proof. The beauty here is that later, if you decide to run ads, you can ask Facebook to build 'lookalike' audiences (with similar tastes and profiles to those that follow your page) that you can also target with those ads.

Facebook's advice is that you typically need 1,000 followers to get the most out of this, but you can try with lower follower numbers. Either way, having a decent sized warm audience that you can target should help make any ad more relevant from the get-go and therefore hopefully encourage Facebook to show it to more people.

Note: If you widen a boost to include Instagram, which Facebook may encourage you to do, there is no way to invite people who react there to like your Facebook page. Thus if you want to run promotions on Instagram I'd do these separately. I talk briefly about Instagram advertising in the next section.

It's easy to follow the instructions on Facebook to boost posts. Just be sure to put a cap on how much you want to spend per day and set a start and end date!

Tip: Unlike with ads, when the audience clicks on your image in a boosted post, it will simply expand that image — it won't take them to your Amazon sales or other landing page. For that reason be sure to include a link to any page you want to promote early on in the text that sits above the fold.

iOS changes affecting Facebook ads from April 2021

As I write, Facebook is updating its guidance around ad targeting, due to changes at Apple.

As I understand it, this will mainly affect the performance of ads that target or build lookalikes from audiences whose details have been imported from outside Facebook and are connected with a Facebook pixel. However, I'm no expert and this may not be the whole story. Search for the latest guidance on Facebook.

Or see this AdEspresso blog post : **bit.ly/FB_ad_changes**

Instagram advertising

At the time of writing, Instagram ads can be run in two ways:

- **As part of a Facebook ad campaign** — you set up the ad in your Facebook ads manager and opt to include Instagram either as one of the placements, or as the only placement. (You need to connect your Instagram business page and your Facebook page in order to do this.)

- **You promote an existing Instagram post** from inside the app on your mobile phone and choose your daily budget there and then.

A couple of things to bear in mind:

- If you run a Facebook ad and include Instagram as a placement, you won't get to use the ideal 30 Instagram hashtags that are so useful for widening reach — your Facebook ad would look pretty awful jam packed with hashtags!

- Instagram placements of Facebook ads don't stay in your Instagram feed, whereas promoted Instagram posts do, so would be permanently visible if someone visits your profile.

I've experimented very briefly with Instagram boosted posts, and didn't see any evidence of increased sales when referring followers to the link in my bio. And on the couple of occasions I included Instagram placements with a Facebook ad, I got a lot of engagement but found no way to invite those people to like my Facebook page. The Facebook help team later confirmed to me that there was no way to do this. All in all not great results!

Where you may have more luck with boosted posts is offering free content in return for an email sign-up.

Bear in mind that I have a tiny Instagram following, so it may be worth running some test posts yourself if you enjoy the platform. However, be very clear about your objective — will it be to sell more books, or simply to grow your following? Given that Instagram is part of the Facebook family I'd be wary of money getting eaten up for no good cause!

As at April 2021 I've still yet to hear of children's authors who say they've made money from Instagram advertising. If that's you, please get in touch and I'll add a case study in the resources area.

As you will have gathered, this isn't my area of expertise. The best advice I can give beyond what's above is search online and read up on best practice and what is working for **children's authors** before being tempted to dip in your toe.

Pinterest advertising

Pinterest allows you to promote your pins in the same way that Facebook allows you to boost posts — and will encourage you to do so on the fly at the time of posting. They also have an ads dashboard from which you can plan campaigns in advance, view detailed analytics and so on. To get full access to analytics you need to set up a business account. You can do this by converting your personal account to one — or you can link your personal account to a separate business account.

Because the *The Secret Lake* was doing well on Amazon, I converted my personal account to a business one and began experimenting with these ads in the summer of 2018, to see if they could help me maintain my Amazon ranking.

I have to confess to finding the dashboard more than confusing, and the path to choosing and monitoring audiences and keywords etc extremely frustrating and unintuitive (on many occasions I got 90% through the process only to find I'd lost all the work I'd just done!). For that reason I rarely go in and tweak the few ads I've set up beyond periodically checking the Costs Per Click (CPC) and Click-Through Rate (CTR). These have remained reasonable (around £0.17 in the UK and $0.20 in the US) and a result I've continued to run low level ads since that time, spending between $/£1.50 and $/£3 a day in those markets. As I don't use affiliate links I've no way of knowing how many of those ads lead to sales — however, they are sending external traffic to my Amazon product pages, which possibly helps keep the algorithms supporting my ads.

Note that once you have a business account you can install a Pinterest 'tag' on your website. As with a Facebook pixel, this is useful if you run ads to your site rather than Amazon as you can potentially retarget those people with news ads. Tags also allow you to create 'actalike' audiences to target. However, bear in mind that iOS changes from Apple as of April 2021 may affect performance of this type of ad. Retargeting is not something I've had time to experiment with, not helped by the fact that, as I mentioned earlier, I find the user experience in the Pinterest ads dash very confusing!

I would suggest experimenting with organic pins and shares to start with and look to advertising once you have the hang of things.

Finally, start small and, as ever, don't spend more than you can afford to lose. You may find that your organic pins serve you well enough.

See Chapter 6 on social media marketing and Pinterest to understand the basics of using Pinterest, and why this platform could be good for children's authors.

To read more about Pinterest advertising, visit their site at **bit.ly/pint_ads**.

BookBub advertising and featured deals

Another platform to be aware of once your book has a decent number of reviews is BookBub, a website that promotes free or discounted **eBooks** to highly targeted (genre specific) lists of avid readers around the world.

BookBub offers two forms of promotion: advertising and featured deals.

BookBub advertising

Authors and publishers can bid to run pay-per-click or pay-per-impression ads to go out with BookBub's newsletters, with the ads linking through to your sales page on your chosen platform. The ads are quick and easy to set up and you can stop and start them at any time. However, these are eBook ads and I'm not sure how relevant they are for books for the under 12s. Also, BookBub doesn't strike me as a natural place that parents would seek out books for their children.

Personally, I'd consider this option pretty low on the list for children's authors unless you have a strong selling middle grade/YA story that you think will appeal to adults, or possibly a middle grade series where you make the first book free or 0.99c/p. After all, we know that *some* children read eBooks — and, given that BookBub customers specify which genre they are looking for, one must assume that those who have signed up for children's books are doing so for a reason.

My hunch is there will be quite a few children's authors in there, seeing how it all works from the customer's viewpoint. However, you may well get your book in front of parents who have signed up on their child's behalf and who then go on to buy the whole series either on Kindle or in print. There's no harm in testing this out.

A few years ago I used BookBub sparingly for *The Secret Lake* to very little avail and at a very high cost-per-click rate. I've been meaning to dip my toe in again since but simply not had the time and (to be honest) feel there are better places to spend my time and money.

Before doing anything, I'd highly recommend reading around on what works and how to avoid wasting money through inefficient targeting or the wrong bid rates. A good place to start is David Gaughran's blog piece **bit.ly/BB_DG**

David also runs a free self-serve starter course on the Reedsy site **bit.ly/bbubads**

Search beyond this also, as things may have moved on by the time you read this.

BookBub featured deals

As alternative to advertising, you can apply for a 'featured deal' to help boost visibility of your book during a price drop. BookBub will include your book in a curated list that it emails to members who have signed up to receive children's or middle grade books.

BookBub describes these as "power readers who often go on to become loyal, long-term fans of the authors they discover on BookBub".

They will also email any readers who've clicked on the book to encourage them to follow the author.

These deals aren't easy to come by — and BookBub *tends* to favour authors whose books are 'wide' rather than in KDP Select. There are certain rules around the discounting that you can read on their website.

The following table shows you the cost of a featured deal at the time of writing. Go to **bit.ly/bbub_prices** for up-to-date info.

BookBub Featured Deal Pricing

		BobBub Fee by Book Price (1 May 2021)					US Stores	
	Subscribers	Free	<$	$1-$2	$2-3	#3+	Free Book Stats	Discounted book stats
Children's	480,000+	$92	$134	$241	$335	$469	4300	400
Middle Grade	470,000+	$92	$134	$241	$335	$469	3800	500

		BobBub Fee by Book Price (1 May 2021)					International	
	Subscribers	Free	<$	$1-$2	$2-3	#3+	Free Book Stats	Discounted book stats
Children's	480,000+	$29	$42	$63	$105	$147	800	80
Middle Grade	470,000+	$29	$42	$63	$105	$147	700	100

		BobBub Fee by Book Price (1 May 2021)					US & International	
	Subscribers	Free	<$	$1-$2	$2-3	$3+	Free Book Stats	Discounted book stats
Children's	480,000+	$121	$176	$304	$440	$616	5100	480
Middle Grade	470,000+	$121	$176	$304	$440	$616	4500	600

Prices at April 2021 - use the link above to check latest rates

Writers of books for adults and YA have had huge success with BookBub featured deals which can have a profound effect on Amazon ranking, especially if run in conjunction with other promos around the same time. However, again, given that this is an eBook tool my gut feeling is that featured deals are probably only worthwhile pursuing if you write in a series for older middle grade children, on the basis that some do read eBooks and their parents may be tempted by a free or 0.99c/p offer to pass on to them and thereafter you may get buy-through. I've not heard of these deals boosting sales of books for younger children but if you have please do let me know! That said, if a $29 featured deal gets more eyes on a new or backlist book for younger children as part of a wider marketing strategy you don't have much to lose!

To understand more about how BookBub marketing works, go to: **support.bookbub.com**

14

EBOOK MARKETING: GO WIDE OR USE KDP SELECT?

When you come to upload your file to the Kindle Store, you will be given the option to enrol in Amazon's 'KDP Select' programme. This means you commit to making your eBook exclusive to Amazon for a period of 90 days and cannot sell it or give it away on any other store or website, including your own. In return, Amazon makes it available through its Kindle Unlimited subscription service, which allows readers to borrow and read unlimited eBooks from its library each month (either on a Kindle, or on other devices using the Kindle App).

With KDP Select, a 'borrow' counts towards your book's Kindle Store ranking and you are paid based on the number of 'page reads' each calendar month. How much you are paid per page read depends on the size of the KDP Fund, announced by Amazon after the end of each month. I assume the fund size is based on the number of Kindle Unlimited subscriptions sold that month and other factors.

The fund proceeds are split between all books enrolled in KDP Select that had page reads. At the time of writing, you are typically paid around 0.0042 cents per page read.

You can view the monthly history of page-read payouts at: **writtenwordmedia.com/2018/05/18/kdp-global-fund-payouts**

Pros and cons of each option

There are both pros and cons of joining KDP Select and this is something you must decide for yourself. Below I set out a few points to consider.

Pros of KDP Select

Crucially, from a marketing perspective, KDP Select members are allowed to set their books 'free' for five days a month and use those days to market it. Any free 'sales' made during that time qualify as 'verified purchases' for review purposes. Many authors use KDP free days to raise the profile of a new book or a back title, as the free downloads often lead to paid sales in the days that follow. I talk more about getting reviews using free days in Chapter 9.

Remember: other than through KDP Select, Amazon doesn't let you price your eBooks as free, even though they may at their discretion price match if you have it free on another store.

Pros of 'going wide' with your eBooks

A key benefit of being 'wide' (ie not opting into KDP Select) — beyond the fact that your eBooks will be available to readers around the world who prefer not to buy from Amazon — is that you'll be able to make your eBooks available to libraries. One of the main ways to do this is via Overdrive, a digital platform that distributes to over 65,000 public libraries, schools, colleges and universities (and companies) in 84 countries worldwide. Another key player is Bibliotheca, which distributes to 30,000 libraries in 20 countries at the time of writing.

Most authors use **Draft2Digital (D2D)** or **PublishDrive** — both global eBook aggregators who both partner with OverDrive — to reach not just the libraries above, but also all the main eBook retailers around the world. D2D takes a 15% cut of your net royalties. PublishDrive has a fixed monthly fee model, and you keep 100% of your royalties.

When signing up to these platforms you can opt out of any online stores where you prefer to upload direct. Opting out if using D2D gives you a higher royalty rate. Thus many authors upload directly to Amazon (but don't choose KDP Select), Kobo, Apple, Google Play (and sometimes Nook Press) then use D2D or PublishDrive for the rest. Another advantage of direct upload on the main stores is that you have access to promotion opportunities on Kobo and Apple that are not always available if you go to them indirectly.

At the time of writing D2D distributes to the stores and library/educational partners below.

- Amazon
- Apple Books
- Barnes & Noble

- Kobo (including Kobo Plus)
- Tolino
- OverDrive
- Bibliotheca
- Scribd
- Baker & Taylor
- Hoopla
- Vivlio

This list will no doubt change over time and you'll find a similar list on PublishDrive. Other distributors include **eBook Partnership** and **Ingram Spark** and by the time you're reading this there may be others. As I say, most authors I know use D2D — and indeed I use it for the eBook version of this title.

None of the above is possible if you're in KDP Select. Whereas a few years ago one might have said this isn't relevant for children's books, we know there has been a shift towards more eBook reading by children during the pandemic. That behaviour *may* stay and *may* grow. Personally, I am also aware of marketing from my local library pointing to their eBooks borrowing service for both adults and children as part of their relationship with Overdrive. And if you delve into Overdrive's site, you start finding microsites such as **Primary and Secondary EBooks Now** whose offering, combined with the Sora reading app, is already in use in UK schools. I am sure the equivalent is on offer for schools in the US and around the world.

A further advantage of being wide is that you can sell your eBooks direct if you wish — for example from a storefront linked to your website. If you choose to do this, make sure the payment platform you use will automatically handle any sales tax for you as this will vary depending on where the customer lives. **Note:** if you're in the UK, whether or not you are VAT-registered, also check whether direct eBook sales into the EU would require special paperwork for VAT reporting. Our usual relationship with Amazon and the major eBook retailers is business to business (B2B) and they are not based in the UK, so those sales are outside the scope of UK VAT. However, if you're selling direct to consumers, registering for 'Non-Union VAT MOSS' may come into play, depending on whether you have a B2B relationship with the storefront handling your sales. I'd recommend checking the detail with an accountant.

Is KDP Select right for you?

This you need to weigh up and decide for yourself. I've moved my books in and out of KDP Select over the years and never sold many eBooks on the other platforms. It's also a bit of an administrative headache to monitor given that most sales are in print in the end.

Others I know who write at the crossover between MG and YA, and who have tried both options, have generally reported that the benefit of page reads outweighs the hassle of going wide.

However, I do know of children's authors who, in the past, found that setting an eBook free on several platforms led to more print sales on Amazon after it price matched and parents tried the eBook for free before buying in print for their children. This strategy may be something to consider to help boost sales if they are flagging, especially if you write in a series.

The above said, if you're planning to run Amazon ads, my personal view is that you're probably better off 'in' than out of KDP Select to start with at least (whether or not you use their free promotion days), as I my hunch is that 'algorithmic merchandising' may work in your favour as Amazon tries to gain more subscribers to Kindle Unlimited. Whether that's a good or bad thing is another question but, at the end of the day, selling children's books is difficult if you're an unknown author without the backing of a publisher's marketing department. This is further compounded by the fact that the buyer isn't your reader.

You can, of course, move out of KDP Select after 90 days if you're not happy with the results. In fact, the word is that if you email them to ask to be released sooner they usually oblige!

For the last few years, Amazon has become my marketing department and I believe (but can't prove) that KDP Select has helped in some way on that front. Ironically — and happily — this marketing effort has also indirectly led to more print sales for bookshops, and that can only be a good thing! I may, however, experiment with moving one or two of my illustrated chapter books out of Select this year to see whether this leads to library borrows. I'll report back on results via my newsletter if I implement this.

Search for **KDP Select** on Amazon for more information.

15

AUDIOBOOK MARKETING

I cover the options and practicalities of self-publishing children's audiobooks in *How to Self-publish and Market a Children's Book (Second Edition),* which came out at the same time as this book. This chapter is aimed at those who already have audiobooks out.

If you're just starting to look at this area I will say, in brief, that the route taken by most authors I know is to use ACX on a non-exclusive basis to distribute to Audible, Amazon and Apple, combined with Findaway Voices for wider distribution. If you google this as a topic you'll find plenty of reading. Note that Findaway Voices has a special deal with Apple, which means that even though ACX distributes there if you're using them, the Findaway Voices instance of your book will override the ACX one and you'll get better royalties from those Findaway sales.

Back to marketing — the audiobook market is evolving rapidly as I write in April 2021, so expect to find more opportunities than those below when you come to read this, and be sure to search online.

Selling or giving away your audiobook direct

Whether you use Findaway Voices or have a non-exclusive deal with ACX you also have the freedom to sell your audiobooks direct. Until recently this was all well and good, but finding a way for readers to *consume* the audiobook was an issue, because, in order to do so, they need an app with inbuilt functionality that:

- remembers where the listener has reached when they stop listening — allowing them to carry on from where they left off
- allows customers to view and skip back and forth through chapters, change the reading speed, jump back or forward 15/30 seconds and so on

A single MP3 audiobook file doesn't offer these options — you're taken back to the start of the file after you stop listening and close your browser. I first realised this in 2016 when I tried giving away my first audiobook — a recording of *Henry Haynes and the Great Escape* — which I made under a non-exclusive 'Pay per project' deal with ACX. While Audible, Apple and Amazon were marketing the fully functioning audiobook, I had only a series of separate MP3s which, even when woven back together into one file, didn't behave like an audiobook!

Happily there are solutions for this now, the most significant being via **BookFunnel** which has a **free downloadable audiobook app which doubles up for eBook reading**. Coupled with BookFunnel's simple audiobook delivery system, the app enables you to **sell or give away your audiobook direct** from your website, newsletter or social media account — you just need to provide a link. You can even offer 'bundles' of audiobooks that they will deliver separately or alongside eBooks! The choice is yours. You also have the option to sell or give away MP3 files, which some customers want.

You need to be on BookFunnel's Mid List plan ($100 a year at the time of writing) or higher to be able to offer audiobooks via BookFunnel. You keep all of your income, aside from any fees charged by the payment provider. See below for more on payment handling.

For children's authors I think the initial most exciting thing is being able to give away or sell discounted copies of your audiobook direct to your email subscribers or website visitors as part of a wider marketing strategy. Skip back to Chapter 11 for a reminder of how landing pages work on BookFunnel for eBooks — the same principle applies for audiobooks.

Payment handling

For payment processing you can keep it simple, eg with PayPal buttons or Payhip links on your webpages or newsletters — or you can go one step further and set up a store front. BookFunnel has teamed up with a number of sales platforms to handle payments — and in some cases sales tax — for you, each with various pros and cons and differing degrees of ease of use. At the time of writing these are: Payhip, Selz, Shopify, WooCommerce and PayPal, though this of course may change. Find out more at **bit.ly/BFselling** or search 'BookFunnel audiobooks' online. (If you are in the UK, check with an accountant if there are any special Non-Union VAT MOSS reporting rules for direct sales to EU customers. *As I understand it* this could apply if you don't have a Business to Business relationship with your payment platform, even if you're not VAT registered. However, I am not an accountant, so may have this wrong.)

Audiobook promo codes

Both AXC's 'exclusive' plan and Findaway Voices provide free promo codes for use at launch or during other marketing drives to help encourage sales. You won't earn royalties for these sales but they do offer a way for you to get early or additional reviews at launch or further down the line. *(However, reading between the lines, if you uploaded your audiobook to ACX and received codes before March 2020 they may still pay royalties on those sales — it's worth checking this.)*

Chirp audiobook promotions

Findaway Voices has partnered with Chirp — a non-subscription audiobook retailer and discovery site set up by the team at BookBub, the hugely successful eBook discovery email marketing platform.

Chirp offers time-limited audiobook deals to curated email lists that readers sign up to (with Kids and YA included in the genres). The audiobooks are delivered through its free audiobook app.

At the time of writing in April 2021, you must be with Findaway in order to market with Chirp (you can opt in during Findaway set-up). Chirp is only available to readers in the US and Canada as I write, and their featured deals that authors can apply for are temporarily free. It's a fast-moving world, so expect any of this to change!

Find out more at **chirpbooks.com**

Findaway Voices extra marketing features

Findaway offers the following additional promotional tools:

- **A separate website 'Authors Direct'** where you can set up a storefront to sell direct and earn 70% of your RRP on each sale. As above, customers download the free Authors Direct app to listen to your book.

- **Priority marketing through 'Voices Plus'** — a program that you can opt into on a title-by-title basis if you commit to use Findaway as your exclusive distributor for that book. In return you get additional extras such as piracy protection, extra promo codes and priority marketing opportunities. *NB This would restrict you from selling your book direct from your own website where you can earn 100% royalties (less processing fees).*

Audiobook sites accepting self-published titles

Glassboxx (UK)

Glassboxx offers another way to sell your audiobook direct. It has a free downloadable app and will manage delivery and sales of your audiobook, pointing customers to the app once they buy. With its default Vendor+ plan it creates a unique landing page for each of your audiobooks, and handles delivery and payments while you do the marketing. There is no annual or monthly fee — rather Glassboxx takes 20% commission from your net income after VAT/sales tax and payment processing fees have been applied. It is allowing free Giveaways at no charge until the end of 2021, thereafter a flat fee of £0.50 per free delivery is expected to be introduced. Glassboxx works with some of the major UK publishing houses — all of whom work on this same royalty split basis. Glassboxx collects and pays over any VAT/ sales tax due for customers based outside of the UK. To me, this implies a business-to-business relationship, so no need for Non-Union VAT MOSS reporting by you. However, I'm not accountant, so do check!

Find out more at **Glassboxx.com**

Cloudaloud audiobook subscription for kids

A relatively new 'kid' on the audio block (excuse the pun!) is **Cloudaloud**, an audiobook streaming app initially designed for children up to age 12, and now with a complementary offering for teens/YA. The app's aim is to promote literacy through audiobooks by helping children find and listen to their known favourites and discover new ones — which may in turn lead to them wanting the book in print or eBook format.

Cloudaloud is only in the UK as I write and only available on iOS. However, it plans to expand to Android later in 2021 and has Europe followed by the US on its roadmap.

The monthly subscription (taken out by parents/other adults) to the app library is currently £3.99 after an initial two-week free trial. Children can browse by genre or age range within a 'safe, walled garden' set-up — away from external advertising or any means for them to run up bills on adult credit cards. If a child enjoys the audiobook enough to want it in print, there is a password protected 'buy button' that links to Cloudaloud's online bookshop where the adult account holder can order it. The buy button only appears where the print book is in stock at Gardners. Looking at the website, in some cases there may also be the opportunity to buy the eBook version.

Cloudaloud hosts a range of children's audiobooks from traditional and small independent publishers, as well as from selected self-published authors. They pay a royalty of 50% of net receipts from the overall subscription revenue pool (after delivery and related costs) — apportioned on a 'per minute listened to' basis. This means that if a child listens to your audiobook twice, you get paid twice for those minutes. This is similar to how KDP Select operates, but without the exclusivity clause and with the added bonus of payments for repeat listens.

Cloudaloud will consider audiobook submissions from self-published authors who have a good sales track record -

though they stress that production values must be top-notch to match content already available. They also say that if they fall in love with a book from a publisher (of any size including self-published), but there is no existing audiobook format, they will consider recording at their expense on a case-by-case basis. In this case the royalty rate drops from 50% to 20% to enable them to recoup up-front costs.

Contract terms for distribution on Cloudaloud on a non-exclusive basis are three years, with a six-month break clause, but may be subject to further negotiation.

At the time of writing, submissions enquiries should go to: mmr@cloudaloud.co.uk

Find out more at **cloudaloud.co.uk**

Pointing ads to your audiobook

At the time of writing, Amazon doesn't allow us to run ads to our audiobooks — but don't be surprised if that changes.

You could, however, target Facebook Ads or social media posts at, for example, parents and grandparents who like audiobooks (chosen from 'interests' when defining your audience) then send them to any of the following:

- your Amazon / Audible / Apple or other retail site landing page
- your audiobook sales page on your website
- your BookFunnel own branded audiobook landing page

- your Authors Direct storefront page on Findaway Voices if you have one (see earlier)
- your Payhip or other direct sales store

See Chapter 13 for more about Facebook advertising.

It would also seem to make sense to word your ad to emphasise the benefits of audiobooks for long journeys, holidays, bedtime routine etc — and to highlight ease of listening options via smart speakers, tablets and mobile phones, with or without headphones.

16

TRANSLATIONS AND FOREIGN RIGHTS

Translation and foreign rights opportunities have opened right up for self-published authors in the last couple of years in particular. Below I give some context, as well as practical tips for managing translations if this is something you wish to pursue as part of your marketing strategy. I cover licensing (selling) Foreign Rights.

Managing your own translations

In the last 18 months, I've managed translation of two titles into a foreign language: French and German editions of *The Christmas Tree Wish* in 2019, and a German edition of *The Secret Lake* in the autumn of 2020. I share my insights below.

Why translations have become a viable option

A key game-changer in the last couple of years if you're looking to have your books translated has been the launch of Amazon Advertising for KDP authors on key non-English language sites. At the time of writing, beyond the US, UK, Australia and Canada (which, of course, has a substantial French-speaking population), you can also run ads in Germany, France, Italy and Spain.

The back-end ads dashboard for each territory is identical to the English language one, and if you have the Chrome translation extension you can flip between the source language and English to keep track of what you're doing, understand keyword choices and so on. You can also use the Chrome extension to research and understand category names, then contact KDP by email to request additional categories as you would for the English language version.

Is translation right for your book?

I've taken very gradual steps in this direction (starting with the picture books was deliberate due to their short length, to test the process) and would recommend doing the same. In short, I'd say only consider this route if **all** of the following apply:

- your book is already selling in good numbers in the UK and/or USA/CA and you are making a profit from it — whether it's standalone or in a series
- it's not so niche in its theme that an overseas audience couldn't relate to it
- you have enough budget and cashflow to pay for the translation, editor and proofreader — and advertising
- you can afford to 'lose' that money if sales don't take off

I'd also say you have the best chances of making sales **where you can already see sales of the English language edition in that country's store,** so think carefully before committing to a project.

Use a professional translator

It goes without saying that if you decide to have your book translated you **must** do so professionally. Please don't ask a Spanish friend who has time to spare, no matter how well read he or she is! I have a degree in French, and completed the most part of a post-graduate Diploma in French to English Translation with City University back in the day, where I gained a distinction for my business translation paper (I've been a professional copywriter for over 30 years) but also did many literary papers as part of the coursework. A lot of hard work and practice is needed, and what you learn when translating literature is just how important nuance and voice is when retelling someone's story. This is not something that comes naturally to someone who isn't already a writer and experienced in literary translation — plus there are conventions to understand and follow when it's not possible to translate concepts like for like.

Translator fees and terms

Here are a few things worth knowing:

- Translators will normally quote a flat fee based on the number of words (this will be based on the word count of the destination work if it's estimated it will be longer).
- Under traditional publishing contracts translators

normally receive an advance and ongoing royalties. When negotiating with you they may ask for a higher fee in return for no royalty share.
- 'Work for hire' contracts will typically assign the copyright to you with no payment of royalties. For self-published authors, this is your aim — even though you may need to pay a higher fee for it.
- In certain countries the law says that copyright of a translated work always belongs with the translator. However this doesn't stop you agreeing a contract that gives you the exclusive license to market the work in all forms in perpetuity.

Tip: If non-payment of royalties isn't legally possible I have heard of a workaround whereby the translator retains the copyright, accepts the higher fee then agrees to a peppercorn royalty that isn't worth either side paying or collecting. As I'm not a lawyer I'll leave it at that — but it may help you in your own negotiations. (Apparently it was a translator who came up with this solution!)

How to find a professional translator

There are a few ways to find translators and editors. I've used all three.

1. Use Reedsy's marketplace

Here you can search by language and children's book sub-genre for an experienced and vetted translator.

The beauty of using Reedsy is that the contract side of things is taken care of for you. In many cases you take your translator on a 'work for hire' basis, which means you will own the copyright and don't need to worry about royalties down the line. The translator will also often be able to find you an editor and proofreader — or you can search for foreign editors on Reedsy. Reedsy takes a 10% fee each from the author and translator.

Where translators require royalties, that's for you to negotiate with them under special conditions that you add into Reedsy's contract.

My editor for *The Secret Lake* came through Reedsy and was able to recommend a proofreader she works with regularly.

Find out more at **Reedsy.com** (Remember: if you sign up via **reedsy.com/a/inglis** you'll get a $20 discount off your first project.)

2. Search online for translators of children's books like yours

I found my German translator for *The Secret Lake* after scouring Amazon.de pages for translators of children's books with a similar theme to my story. I also researched German literary translator associations websites for more options before making my final choice — it turned out my translator was a member of one of those organisations.

Google brings up translator associations for each of the different countries and it's a matter of drilling into them then making contact with anyone that looks a good fit. You will then need to negotiate terms and sign a contract — many will have a template that you can use as your starting point.

3. Use personal recommendations

As more self-published authors commission translations, expect to be able to get word-of-mouth recommendations. I found my translator for *The Christmas Tree Wish ('Martin le Sapin de Noël)* through a personal recommendation. I then used a French freelance specialist agency for editing and proofreading after double checking the agency's credentials.

Other options

There are other online platforms such as **Babelcube**, which offers a translator/author matching service in 15 languages, based on no up-front fee and a royalty share agreement. I discounted this because I don't want to get into the long-term commitment of royalty share. Also, Babelcube locks you into a five-year book distribution contract and uses their own ISBNs, which means you're not the publisher of record. I was also concerned about how experienced a translator would be if they were happy to work for no fee or guarantee of sales.

That said, I appreciate that this could be a great way for newly qualified translators to cut their teeth. You are able to check authors' reviews of their work and, of course, you could search for the translator's name on Amazon to read star reviews against their work. However, having another company publish my translation and only indirect access to sales data is a deal-breaker for me personally.

If you can't find someone through your own research, I'd recommend using Reedsy. Their vetting service, by the way, means they accept only five percent of the translators who apply to join their list.

READING RESOURCES

How to read a translation rights contract: Alliance of Independent Authors — gives tips on what to expect/look out for in a contract. Free to ALLi members — log on to the website and search under 'Contracts'.

If you're a member of the Society of Authors, or equivalent in your country, check their database for sample translation contracts. There will be things in there to learn from.

Licensing foreign rights

Licensing foreign rights (or 'selling foreign rights') means you grant an overseas publisher the exclusive right to translate, print, publish and sell your book in a given language and in a given territory or territories for an agreed period. The contract sets out which formats are covered (one or more of paperback, hardback, eBook, audiobook etc) and the advance, initial print run and ongoing royalties that will be paid in respect of each of those formats.

Approaches from foreign publishers or agents

In the last couple of years I, and several other high selling self-published children's authors I know, have signed foreign rights deals after receiving direct enquiries from overseas publishers. The contracts I have signed have all been in languages where managing the translation myself would have been an 'indie step too far' as I have no knowledge of the language. As I write, I've signed with Albania, Russia, Czech Republic, Iran, Ukraine, Turkey and China — with the first four in this list on sale as I write.

The initial approach and conversation tends to go like this:

- The publisher or overseas agent emails requesting a PDF reading copy of your book. Any agent will normally quote the name of the publisher client.

- At this stage, check credentials online. If you can't find a website, or if the website you find feels shady or simply looks like an online store filled with poorly designed book covers, google Victoria Strauss 'Writer Beware' to see if the company name comes up as untrustworthy to deal with. It can be flattering to receive these emails, but you need to keep things in perspective. If still in doubt, ask in writer Facebook groups and/or contact the Alliance of Independent Authors or Society of Authors to see if they know of them. (For the most part, the publishers I've signed with had a string of recognisable traditionally published children's books on their lists.)

- If the publisher is legitimate, send them a low resolution PDF reading copy.

- Several weeks may now pass by. After this, if they are interested they will email with an initial 'in principle' offer, usually comprising a proposed advance, royalty rate (by format if they're looking for more than print), initial print run, and contract term.

- Be ready to negotiate these high level terms after getting advice (see next point). If you all agree, they would then send you a draft contract with the full details for review.

- For the high level offer — and most certainly the detailed contract terms — I would consult with an expert in foreign rights licensing. Both the Alliance of Independent Authors and Society of Authors (SoA) offer a free contracts vetting service for members. Take advantage of this. (I'm a member of both and have used The SoA of late and have found their response times to be excellent. As they work with many traditional authors, I figure they will have their finger on the pulse of what constitutes a typical and reasonable offer from a given territory — and what doesn't! Otherwise, ALLi has partnered with a literary agency that offers rights advice.)

Key things to look out for in any contract you sign

- Automatic rights reversion if the publisher goes into liquidation
- Rights reversion if the publisher fails to pay on time/as agreed
- Publisher does not have the right to sub-licence or

transfer the work to another publisher without your permission*

- Can't make the eBook free or publish it on their website — ie it must be a separate digital eBook that is paid for and subject to royalties (free sample is okay) — I'd say the same for the audio
- Must produce the Print book before the eBook — I'd probably say ditto for the audiobook, though I only have one deal with audio and didn't think to ask this at the time
- eBook must be securely encrypted etc
- 6-monthly or yearly reports of sales by each format inc RRP
- For the avoidance of doubt, clarify that no other format not mentioned in the contract is part of the agreement (eg film or any other formats that may not yet exist!)
- Publisher to inform you of each print run date and quantities / RRP
- None of the formats to be combined with other works
- If the print work becomes unavailable for sale through the usual channels, you have the right to ask for the rights back and this must be granted within six months of your request (or they put it back on sale)
- For the avoidance of doubt, print on demand format does not constitute the print version being available for sale
- No ads to appear in your book, and no illustrations you didn't have in there originally

- True and faithful unabridged translation etc
- Free copies sent to you etc
- Try to say they will cover bank fees for advance and royalty payments — though in practice this doesn't always work!

*Ask your contracts reviewer to include a clause covering your rights/royalty payments if the publisher is acquired. Some authors of bestselling movie books have stopped receiving royalties after Disney acquired the original publisher and argues they inherited the publisher's assets but not its debts. There is a huge movement trying to rectify this. It seems to me that a clause is needed stating that if the publishing company is sold and royalties discontinue, the contract becomes void. Search **#disneymustpay** to read the latest on this.

Note: *I am not a lawyer: get advice from ALLi, the SoA (or equivalent in your country), and/or a publishing contracts lawyer.*

Approaching overseas publishers

In earlier years, I had tried approaching overseas publishers who I thought were a good fit for my books, but never with any success. My starting point was the foreign rights catalogues from London Book Fair and Bologna Children's Book Fair - search online. It is a laborious and thankless task — best left to an experienced agent in my view! If you're determined, you'll need to find publishers with lists that fit your genre and query them by phone and/or email.

Approaching foreign rights agents

If you are selling extremely well but don't want to manage your own translations, it may be worth researching foreign rights agents or agencies who would be prepared to represent you. They may be few and far between, and your book would need to fit their catalogues, but you won't know if you don't try! An easy place to start would be by asking in Facebook and other groups of established self-published children's authors — you may find some bestsellers there who have done deals this way. You could also search on the Reedsy listing for children's Literary Agents.

- You can view Reedsy's list at **bit.ly/kidsagents**
- Also take a look at **publishersmarketplace.com** where you may be able to glean a few contacts without having to subscribe.
- And / or search 'foreign rights agents children's books' online.

Foreign rights agents typically take a 15% percentage cut from your advance and royalty. If they work with an overseas 'co-agent' to secure you a deal, the fee typically rises to 20%, split between the two. Get advice from a contracts expert before signing.

Recommended Reading

How Authors Sell Publishing Rights: ALLi's Guide to Working with Publishers, Producers and Others — due out in 2021 (search online). Free to ALLi members via their website, or buy online.

17

CHILDREN'S BOOK AWARDS OPEN TO SELF-PUBLISHED AUTHORS

One way you can help raise your book's profile is by winning an award (or being placed in the runners up or finalist shortlist), as this offers the chance for PR, winner stickers and more.

Yes, that's easier said than done — but you can't win if you don't try!

Overleaf you'll find example awards that are open to self-publishers and accept children's books. These have been checked and recommended as 'safe' by the Alliance of Independent Authors. Beyond this, I'd say 'buyer beware'. You may come across other awards, or receive marketing emails encouraging you to enter a specialist award — but take care. Some come with high fees and/or such a high number of categories that their key aim appears to be making money over and above highlighting great children's books.

Children's book awards vetted by the Alliance of Independent Authors

- **The Wishing Shelf Book Awards** — thewsa.co.uk
- **The International Rubery Awards** — ruberybookaward.com
- **The Kindle Storyteller Awards** — search online
- **The Eric Hoffer Award** — hofferaward.com

Not on the list as I write, but expect to see added:

- **The Selfies Awards: separate for UK and US**
- **US** — selfiesbookawards.com
- **UK** — theselfies.co.uk

(This list may be updated over time, so do check.)

If you are contemplating entering any other award, check ALLi's list first using the link below. ALLi rates most of the awards that are out there with commentary on whether to proceed with caution: **bit.ly/selfpubawards**

If this page should move at any future date, search for *Alliance of Independent Authors award and content ratings.*

In 2016 I entered The Wishing Shelf Book Awards — where *Walter Brown and the Magician's Hat* was a Red Ribbon Winner (essentially a runners up award) — and would highly recommend it. Not only is your book read and voted on by children and teachers in UK primary schools, but you can also pay a small amount extra at entry to receive a written report on what did and didn't work, no matter where you come in the competition. I regret not discovering this award sooner. Had I done so, I certainly would have entered *The Secret Lake* and *Eeek! The Runaway Alien.*

In 2019 I entered the UK Selfies Award, where *The Christmas Tree Wish* was shortlisted in the children's category. Sadly, *The Tell-Me Tree* didn't make it to the last six in 2020 — but I know several authors (for adult and children's books) whose books did!

18

STRATEGIC MARKETING TIPS FOR CHILDREN'S AUTHORS

To round off, below is a very quick list of tips that may help you sell more books. Not all are unique to children's books, and some I have covered already.

At-a-glance checklist

- Write a series — if you hook the reader in with book one they will come back for more. This is especially the case with children's books.
- If you don't have a series, aim to write to the same age group and include an excerpt from one of your other books in your back matter.
- If you write across a range of age groups, turn it to your advantage — you have the opportunity to offer to see more pupils/classes at school visits. Also,

most young children have siblings — so be sure to include the target age range when promoting your other books in your back matter.

- If you have several standalone books, consider creating an eBook sampler that's not in KDP Select and include the first chapter of each. Make this 99c/99p on Amazon and free on all other stores then contact Amazon and ask them to price match. I've done this with ***Story Stack*** — search online.

- Within the above eBook, include links to each individual book's sales pages — and a link to sign up to your email list.

- Offer something for free from your website or back/front of your books to encourage email sign-up and/or to hook new readers into your books. This might be a short story prequel to one of your books, a character's diary entry, or a quiz or puzzle that relates to the *theme* of your book. For younger audiences, it could be downloadable colouring sheets. Include the book title and URL of your website in the footer of all free downloads. If these freebies get passed around it could lead to more sales. (Adding the link at the front of the book as well as the back may get more eyes on it.)

- Write curriculum related activities or lesson plans related to your book(s) and promote them to teachers via social media, ads, and/or on your website — possibly encouraging sign-up to a newsletter at the same time. Make these free or paid, depending on their complexity.

- Read up on how to select the most appropriate initial two categories for your book on Amazon to make it discoverable — covered at: **bit.ly/KDPCatHelp**

- Be sure to include the age range and US grade range when setting up your book page on Amazon, as these further improve discoverability. Use the link above for more info. NB this page previously also included 'required keywords' to fit in certain children's book sub-categories — eg the word 'extraterrestrial' was needed to feature in the children's book sub-category that includes aliens. At the time of writing, that information is no longer there so I can only assume these 'mandatory' keywords no longer apply. If in doubt, email KDP's helpdesk and ask!

- Make the most of the fact that you can ask to be included in up to eight more categories in the Amazon Kindle Store and the same in the Books store (ie 10 in total per store). Once you've identified the best categories for your book (see below for tools to help you with this), use the 'Contact us' button within KDP to call or email your requests. Do this for as many stores as possible and, at the very least, the UK, USA and Canada and any other site where you are advertising, or starting to see sales. See the end of this section for tools to help with category research.

- Don't be tempted to opt for unsuitable categories just for the sake of inclusion, or to try to win a 'bestseller' badge. This will confuse the Amazon algorithms, which may start recommending your book to unsuitable audiences and then downgrade its visibility in searches if sales don't follow.

- Read up on how to make your book blurb and Amazon page description compelling — listen to the **Indie Kidlit Podcast Episode 30 with Bryan Cohen** and search online for more interviews with him. I'd also recommend *Amazon Blurbs Unleashed* by Robert J Ryan who, like me, has a strong copywriting background. Test with trusted readers/writers. If you're stuck, take a look at Bryan Cohen's *Best Page Forward* service, or hire someone to help with you.

- Use Dave Chesson's free KindlePreneur tool to format your book descriptions at upload — see last section.

- Consider offering virtual author visits beyond your county, state or country. See Chapter 5.

- Make **relevancy** your watchword when advertising — for keywords, categories, and audience targeting. See more in Chapter 13.

- Once you have an established sales track record and testimonials from school visits, search online for organisations in your country that connect schools with authors. Most say they won't accept self-published authors, but they will make exceptions. In the UK I am listed with the website *Contact An Author* — this was after three years into my school visits programme.

- Upload excerpts or retail samples from any audiobooks you have out to SoundCloud and embed them into websites and newsletters for an instant listening experience. Or do the same using BookFunnel — see Chapter 15 on audiobook marketing to find out more.

- Claim and set up your Author page on as many sites as are available. See my and other author pages to get an idea of what to include. The instructions for how to set the page up are clear — just look for the link on your book's sales page once it appears on Amazon. Make the most of the opportunity to add links to your blog and social media.

- If you decide not to be in KDP Select, create an eBook version of your standalone title or first in a series and list it for free on all the main eBook sites and at 0.99p / 0.99c on Amazon. Contact Amazon via the Help page in your KDP dashboard and ask them to price match. I'd probably include one or two links to show them where it's selling for free. Several children's authors I know have reported success with crossover sales to print using this strategy. KDP will usually price match.

- Set up a shop page on **Bookshop.org** and sign up for their affiliate programme. Include links to your shop from your website and emails, to attract print book buyers who want to support local independent bookshops. Search online to learn more.

- Consider selling eBooks, audiobooks or signed books direct from a storefront page on or linked to your website. Be sure to choose a payment platform that takes care of any sales tax or EU VAT. (If you are based in the UK, check the rules around VAT reporting of Business to Consumer sales of digital goods to the EU and elsewhere.)

Recommended reading on discoverability

Good places to start if you want to understand more about the principles of discoverability and category choice are *Let's Get Digital* and *Amazon Decoded* by David Gaughran. His other book *Strangers to Superfans* is also recommended for further on in your marketing journey. His key messages — that asking friends and family to buy your book and/or placing your title in irrelevant categories in order to get a 'bestseller' tag are **not** ways to get your book noticed on Amazon (and indeed can positively harm its performance) — are always at the forefront of my mind when planning my marketing.

Popular tools to help with keyword and category selection

The tools below were extremely helpful to me when first setting up Amazon ads, and although I now tend to 'hand-pick' my keywords, identifying suitable categories using Publisher Rocket is extremely quick and easy. For category analysis alone it's worth the one-off fee in my view.

If you can't stretch to that, try BKLNK.com, free at the time of writing and with no apparent plans to charge beyond donations. BKLNK also has a feature that gives you the top 50 ASINS (identifier codes) for books in a given category — this is useful for Keyword ads that target individual Products by ASIN. But, again, be sure to check and remove irrelevant titles.

- **Publisher Rocket — $97 —** bit.ly/RocketKarenInglis
- **Kindle Spy — $47**
- **BKLNK.com — free with the option to donate**

Prices as at March 2021, excluding VAT. *(Disclosure: the above is an affiliate link at no extra cost to you.)*

Popular tool to format book descriptions for Amazon and other online sites

Use Dave Chesson's free Book Description Generator to format your text before uploading to Amazon, Kobo and Barnes & Noble. *(Disclosure: this is an affiliate link should you later choose to buy Publisher Rocket.)*

- **bit.ly/DC_Format**

19

WRITING AND SELF-PUBLISHING GROUPS AND WEBSITES

The self-publishing world is renowned for its generosity. Support from other children's writers and the wider self-publishing community can be a lifeline when you're struggling to understand why something isn't working, need best-practice tips, are looking for feedback on book covers or descriptions, want advice on courses or other paid services, and much more. Below are self-publishing organisations, groups, website and podcasts that I recommend.

Organisations

The Alliance of Independent Authors *(ALLi)*

The leading global professional association for authors who self-publish and which brings together the world's best indie authors, advisors and self-publishing services. ALLi champions professionalism in self-publishing and actively campaigns to protect, promote and further the interests of independent authors in the publishing world. Once you join you get access to its closed Facebook page, which you can drop into at any time to search for advice or ask a question. ALLi members enjoy fee waivers with Ingram Spark.

If you decide to join, please consider using the affiliate link **bit.ly/ALLiKaren** — I'll earn a small referral fee, but it won't cost you more. Thank you!

allianceindependentauthors.org

Society of Children's Book Writers and Illustrators *(SCBWI)*

A great networking organisation for children's authors including traditionally published, unpublished/looking for a traditional deal, and self-published. Headquarters are in the US but it has very active 'chapters' and Facebook pages in many countries including the UK, and annual conferences in the US and UK that are jam-packed with practical guidance on children's book writing and marketing. You don't need to be a member to attend the conferences.

SCBWI.org

Websites and podcasts for children's authors

Darcy Pattison

US children's author Darcy Pattison is both traditionally and self-published. As well as writing for children, she runs children's writing workshops and retreats. Visit her website for a wealth of information including periodic deep dives into the technical side of self-publishing. Darcy also has an online course on how to write and self-publish a children's picture book. She is a tech wizard, has won awards for her non-fiction picture books, and knows bucket loads about supplying to libraries and schools. **darcypattison.com**

Laurie Wright

Based in Canada, Laurie is a successful children's picture book author and publishing coach, best known for her 'Mindful Mantra' picture books series. You will find her podcast at **bit.ly/lauriewrightpodcast**, her author website at **lauriewright.com** and her training courses for novices upwards at **bit.ly/LWrightResources** *Note:* I've not taken any of Laurie's courses so can't vouch for them on that basis. However, given her long-term success they are worth a look if you're struggling with your marketing. Many are priced at $49 or below. There may be something in there for you to set you in the right direction.

Stacy Bauer

American picture book author Stacy Bauer has always generously shared her self-publishing journey in Facebook groups — including around organising Kickstarter campaigns to fund up-front print runs. More recently, she has put together a range of bite-sized courses to support other children's authors who write for this younger age range. Again, I've not taken any of these so can't vouch for them personally but based on the information she has shared in groups I'm sure they will offer on-point practical help if you need handholding in certain areas. You can navigate to her courses from her website **stacycbauer.com**

• • •

Self-publishing Adventures website

As you will know, this is my own website, started back in 2011 soon after I began my self-publishing journey. It focuses on the practicalities of self-publishing and marketing children's books at a high level, with a focus on print on demand. A place to refer others looking for free guidance who may not be ready to buy this book. **selfpublishingadventures.com**

Websites and podcasts: self-pub general

Self-publishing Advice — Alliance of Independent Authors (ALLi)

This is the free advice blog of ALLi and is not to be missed. You don't have to be a member of ALLi to access the articles but you do need to be if you want to write for the blog or be featured. The blog is filled with indispensable guidance on all aspects of self-publishing, broken down into handy sections. Use search to bring up specific children's book articles. **selfpublishingadvice.org**

The Creative Penn website and podcast

Self-publishing guru Joanna Penn's jam-packed website is full of free advice on self-publishing fiction and non-fiction, plus articles, interviews, free downloads, videos, and free and paid-for training. She also hosts a regular podcast. Search 'children's books' on the site to focus on our genre — there's lots in there.

thecreativepenn.com

Self-publishing Formula website and podcast

Thriller writer Mark Dawson and his team offer a wealth of free guidance on self-publishing, as well as highly regarded paid-for online courses that have changed many authors' lives. A great resource for beginners and seasoned self-publishers alike, with access to a closed Facebook community group for mailing list members. Its scope is much wider than children's books, but it is not to be missed. **selfpublishingformula.com**

20

WHERE NEXT FOR BOOK MARKETING?

Without a doubt, the opportunities for book marketing have evolved in favour of children's authors in the last few years — with, as we have seen, many of the enhanced Amazon advertising features previously offered only to traditional publishers now available to self-publishers. Until that happened, we had to rely almost exclusively on face-to-face events for selling our books because discoverability online was so difficult. Thank you, Amazon!

The pandemic of 2020/21 has been difficult for us all. However, it has encouraged many more schools and bookclubs to embrace virtual events, opening up much wider possibilities for children's authors both at home and abroad. As I write, I know we are all craving getting back to face-to-face school visits, but I think virtual visits will be a much more regular part of our marketing mix going forward, as everyone is now at ease with the technology. In fact, I have a virtual visit request for a school in the north of

England next week. That would have been unheard of 18 months ago — everything was face to face here in the UK.

Thanks to all of these changes, we're starting to see indie authors appear in bestseller lists in The Bookseller. *The Secret Lake* and a few more children's titles by self-published authors have popped up there in the last year, and books for adults by L J Ross and Mark Dawson now do so semi-regularly. Both of these authors are now distributing print books in bulk to bookshops in the UK. Mark Dawson's print books are also finding prominent shelf space abroad.

Where foreign editions are concerned, I expect to see not only more licensing through direct approaches, but also more translations, encouraged by the opening up of international advertising on Amazon and the availability of vetted freelance translators on sites such as Reedsy.

I also expect to see more direct selling by authors from their sites — including of audiobooks.

We've come a long way on so may fronts in the (almost) three years since I published the first edition of *How to Self-publish and Market a Children's Book* and I expect that shift to continue forward.

As the traditional and self-publishing worlds continue to collide, I'm hopeful that more ways of working together to create and promote top quality books will evolve, irrespective of route to publication. Needless to say, I include children's books in this mix. I hope that you are as excited as I am to continue to be a part of this changing landscape.

21

RESOURCES AND UPDATES

You will find any downloads that come with this book in a joint resources folder for both this and *'How to Self-publish and Market a Children's Book'* (both editions) at the following hidden link:

selfpublishingadventures.com/resources

The password, which is case sensitive, is **WellSaidPress**.

I shall also use this folder to post news of critical changes in the self-publishing world that affect the currency of this book's content — and to add additional recommended resources that I come across. If you are signed up to my mailing list I shall also email you whenever I post there.

REVIEW AND FEEDBACK

Please leave a short review online

I hope you have found this marketing edition useful, wherever you are in your writing or publishing journey.

It would mean a lot to me if you could leave an honest review online — however short — every little helps, as we authors all know.

Thank you!

Feedback

If you want to alert me to a resource or service that you feel deserves a mention in the resources folder for this book, please email me and I'll take a look and get back to you as soon as I can. Ditto for the inevitable typo or error that slips through the net, for which advance apologies!

You can contact me at: kpinglis@wellsaidpress.com

ALSO BY KAREN INGLIS

The Secret Lake (8-11 yrs)

A lost dog, a hidden time tunnel and a secret lake take Stella and Tom to their home and the children living there 100 years in the past. Over 250,000 print copies sold in the English language. In translation in eight languages.

Eeek! The Runaway Alien (7-10 yrs)

A soccer-mad alien comes to Earth for the World Cup! *"Laugh-out-loud funny!"* Loved by keen and reluctant readers alike. Voted favourite book club read three years in a row by boys and girls at one London primary school.

Walter Brown and the Magician's Hat (7-10 yrs)

A boy, a magic top hat and a talking cat spell magical mayhem after Walter Brown inherits his Great Grandpa Horace's magician's hat! *Wishing Shelf Awards* Red Ribbon Winner 2016.

Henry Haynes and the Great Escape (6-8 yrs)

A boy, a magic library book and a bossy boa — oh, and a VERY smelly gorilla with a zoo escape plan! Fun and fast-paced for early readers.

The Tell-Me Tree (4-8 yrs)

'Hello, I am the Tell-Me Tree. Why don't you come and sit by me. Tell me your worries. Tell me your cares. Share your best dreams, or your scary nightmares.'

A gentle rhyming story that invites children to share how they are feeling with friends, family or trusted grown-ups — whether happy, sad, confused, lonely, or anywhere in between. Comes with free printable download activities, for use at home or in the classroom.

The Christmas Tree Wish (3-6 yrs)

As the snow starts to fall on Christmas Eve morning, little Bruce Spruce dreams about finding a home for Christmas Day. But when things don't quite go to plan his fir tree friends rally round to help. A heartwarming tale about hope, friendship and being different. Shortlisted for the UK Selfies Award, 2020.

Ferdinand Fox's Big Sleep (3-5 yrs)

'Ferdinand Fox curled up in the sun, as the church of St Mary struck quarter past one. His tummy was full, he was ready for sleep, and closing his eyes he began to count sheep…'

When Peter Maceever spots Ferdinand Fox sleeping in his garden, he tiptoes out to take a photo. Ferdinand stirs, opens one eye, then goes straight back to sleep! He has far more important things to do — like dream about cake and ice cream! Young children love the rhyming text, the vibrant illustrations inside Ferdinand's dream bubbles, discussing their favourite food, and the counting of time as the church clock strikes from one to five. Based on the true story of a fox that once fell asleep in the author's garden.

Ferdinand Fox and the Hedgehog (3-6 yrs)

'Ferdinand Fox trotted down past the park, where the seesaws and swings stood still in the dark. His magnificent tail sailed along in the light of the streetlamp above, which lit up the night.

That very same night, seeking bugs with her snout, Hatty the hedgehog was out and about. As soon as she smelled the scent of a fox, she scampered to hide in an old soggy box.'

Introducing Hatty the hedgehog and her baby son Ed who meet Ferdinand Fox when out hunting bugs one night. Includes eight pages of photos and fun facts about foxes and hedgehogs. Perfect for little ones.

Order online or from your local bookshop

ABOUT THE AUTHOR

Karen Inglis is an Amazon bestselling children's author who lives in London, England. She has two sons who inspired her to write when they were younger. Karen has presented on children's self-publishing at conferences and masterclasses around the UK and is Children's Advisor at the Alliance of Independent Authors. For her **non-fiction** she writes under the name **Karen P Inglis**.

Sign up to her mailing list at **selfpublishingadventures.com/news** to follow her journey and be notified about **updates or additions to this book.**

Sign up to her children's books mailing list at **kareninglisauthor.com** to be notified about **new children's book releases, events and special offers.**

facebook.com/kareninglisauthor
twitter.com/kareninglis
instagram.com/kareninglis_childrensbooks

ACKNOWLEDGEMENTS

Huge thanks to Catherine Gough, of **FineWords.net**, for her attention to detail and useful comments over so many pages for the first edition of *How to Self-publish and Market a Children's Book,* much of which is still in place in this marketing edition. Equally huge thanks to Robert Selkirk, my copyeditor for this particular edition. Thank you again to Rachel Lawston at **LawstonDesign.com** for the cover concept and design.

Finally, as always, thank you to all my blog followers — and to fellow children's authors and self-publishers in the various online groups to which I belong, and with whom I have exchanged so much know-how over the years. The indie author community is very special, and a place where we continue to learn from each other. I still feel privileged to be a member.